MARCELO BIELSA

Coaching Build Up Play
Against High Pressing Teams

WRITTEN BY
ATHANASIOS TERZIS

PUBLISHED BY

MARCELO BIELSA

Coaching Build Up Play Against High Pressing Teams

First Published June 2017 by SoccerTutor.com

info@soccertutor.com | www.SoccerTutor.com

UK: 0208 1234 007 | **US:** (305) 767 4443 | **ROTW:** +44 208 1234 007

ISBN: 978-1-910491-15-7

Author

Athanasios Terzis © 2017

Edited by

Alex Fitzgerald - SoccerTutor.com

Cover Design by

Alex Macrides, Think Out Of The Box Ltd.
Email: design@thinkootb.com Tel: +44 (0) 208 144 3550

Diagrams

Diagram designs by SoccerTutor.com. All the diagrams in this book have been created using SoccerTutor.com Tactics Manager Software available from www.SoccerTutor.com

Note: While every effort has been made to ensure the technical accuracy of the content of this book, neither the author nor publishers can accept any responsibility for any injury or loss sustained as a result of the use of this material.

CONTENTS

Meet the Author 7

Marcelo Bielsa Coach Profile 8

Marcelo Bielsa's Influence on Top Coaches 9

Marcelo Bielsa's Tactics 10

Marcelo Bielsa's Attacking Philosophy 12

BUILDING UP PLAY AGAINST HIGH PRESSING TEAMS 13

Building Up Play Against High Pressing Teams 14

Requirements for Building Up Play from the Back 15

Coaching Format 16

Key 16

CHAPTER 1: BUILDING UP PLAY FROM THE BACK AGAINST 2 FORWARDS 17

Positioning to Build Up Play Against 2 Forwards 18

STEP 1: Providing a Free Passing Option for the Goalkeeper Against 2 Forwards 19

1a) Creating a 3 v 2 Situation at the Back by Adapting to an Attacking 3-3-3-1 Formation .20

1b) Creating a 3 v 2 Situation at the Back by Adapting to a More Defensive 3-4-3 Formation 22

STEP 2: Moving the Ball to the Target or Free Player Against 2 Forwards 23

2a) Who is the Target Player? 23

2b) Moving the Ball to the Target Player or Free Player 26

2c) Building Up Play and Attacking from the Centre When the 2 Opposition Forwards Force Play Inside 28

SESSION 1: BUILDING UP PLAY AND ATTACKING FROM THE CENTRE 33

SESSION FOR THIS TACTICAL SITUATION (3 Practices)

1. Reading the Tactical Situation to Play the Right Pass When Building Up Play from the Centre 34

2. Reading the Tactical Situation When Building Up Play from the Centre in a Functional Practice 36

3. Reading the Tactical Situation When Building Up Play from the Centre in a Zonal Game .37

CHAPTER 2: MOVING THE BALL TO THE TARGET PLAYER ON THE WEAK SIDE 38

Moving the Ball to the 'Target Player' on the Weak Side 39

Option 1: Pass Back to Goalkeeper Who Acts as a 'Link Player' to Switch the Play 40

Option 2: If the Pass Back to the Goalkeeper is Blocked, the Inside Pass Will Probably Be Free 41

Option 3: Using the Central Midfielder to Switch the Play After Quick Combination Play 42

Option 4: If the Pass Back to GK + Inside Pass Are Blocked, the Full Back Acts as a 'Link Player' to Switch Play.....43

SESSION 2: PLAYING THROUGH PRESSURE ON STRONG SIDE & SWITCH PLAY AGAINST 2 FORWARDS 44

SESSION FOR THIS TACTICAL SITUATION (2 Practices)

1. Pattern of Play to Build Up and Switch the Play Against 2 Forwards 45

2. Playing Through Pressure on Strong Side Against 2 Forwards and Switching Play in an 8 (+GK) v 6 Game 46

SESSION 3: SWITCHING PLAY AND EXPLOITING AN ADVANTAGE ON THE WEAK SIDE (2 FORWARDS).......47

SESSION FOR THIS TACTICAL SITUATION (4 Practices)

1. Pattern of Play to Build Up & Switch Play Against 2 Forwards + Attacking Combinations on Weak Side 48

2. Switching Play Against 2 Forwards and Exploiting an Advantage on Weak Side in a Functional Practice 50

3. Switching Play Against 2 Forwards and Exploiting an Advantage on Weak Side in a Functional Game 52

4. Switching Play Against 2 Forwards and Exploiting an Advantage on Weak Side in an 11 v 11 Zonal Game 53

CHAPTER 3: BUILDING UP PLAY FROM THE BACK AGAINST 1 FORWARD 54

Positioning to Build Up Play Against 1 Forward...55

STEP 1: Providing a Free Passing Option for the Goalkeeper Against 1 Forward 57

STEP 2: Moving the Ball to the Target or Free Player Against 1 Forward 58

SESSION 4: PLAYING THROUGH PRESSURE ON STRONG SIDE & SWITCH PLAY AGAINST 1 FORWARD.......62

SESSION FOR THIS TACTICAL SITUATION (2 Practices)

1. Pattern of Play to Build Up and Switch the Play Against 1 Forward 63

2. Playing Through Pressure on Strong Side Against 1 Forward and Switching Play in an 8 (+GK) v 6 Game.......64

SESSION 5: SWITCHING PLAY AND EXPLOITING AN ADVANTAGE ON THE WEAK SIDE (1 FORWARD).......65

SESSION FOR THIS TACTICAL SITUATION (4 Practices)

1. Pattern of Play to Build Up and Switch the Play Against 1 Forward + Attacking Combinations................66

2. Switching Play Against 1 Forward and Exploiting an Advantage on the Weak Side in a Functional Practice 68

3. Switching Play Against 1 Forward and Exploiting an Advantage on the Weak Side in a Functional Game 70

4. Switching Play Against 1 Forward and Exploiting an Advantage on the Weak Side in an 11 v 11 Zonal Game...71

CHAPTER 4: CREATING AND EXPLOITING 3 v 2 SITUATIONS NEAR THE SIDELINE........72

STEP 3: Creating a Numerical Advantage Near the Sideline 73

STEP 4: Exploiting the Numerical Advantage Created...75

Option 1a: Direct Pass to the Full Back Who is Free of Marking Near the Sideline...............................75

Option 1b: Exploiting the 2 v 1 with the Winger's Run into the Space Behind the Full Back 76

Option 1c: The Winger Exploits the Space Created in the Centre by the Forward's Run Out Wide 77

Option 2: Quick Combination Play to Move the Ball to the Free Full Back when the Direct Pass is Blocked.......78

Option 3: The Winger is Able to Receive in Space and Turn with 2 Passing Options.............................79

Option 4: Exploiting the Space Behind the Opposition Full Back Who Moves Forward to Mark Our Winger.......80

SESSION 6: CREATING AND EXPLOITING 3 v 2 SITUATIONS NEAR THE SIDELINE............................81

SESSION FOR THIS TACTICAL SITUATION (8 Practices)

1. Moving into Available Passing Lanes with Quick Combination Play (Unopposed)............................82

2. Synchronised Movements and Combination Play Between the Full Back and Winger (Unopposed) 83

3. Synchronised Movements and Combination Play Between the Full Back and Winger (Opposed) 84

4. Playing to the Free Player in a 3 v 1 Tactical Situation Near the Sideline 85

5. Playing to the Free Player in a 3 v 2 Tactical Situation Near the Sideline 86

6. Creating and Exploiting a 3 v 2 Numerical Advantage Near the Sideline in a Functional Practice 87

7. Creating and Exploiting a 3 v 2 Numerical Advantage Near the Sideline in an 11 v 10 Game 88

8. Creating and Exploiting a 3 v 2 Numerical Advantage Near the Sideline in an 11 v 11 Game 89

CHAPTER 5: ATTACKING SOLUTIONS WITH A 3 v 3 SITUATION NEAR THE SIDELINE......90

Attacking Solutions with a 3 v 3 Situation Near the Sideline (Against 2 Forwards)............................91

Attacking Solutions with a 3 v 3 Situation Near the Sideline (Against 1 Forward)............................94

SESSION 7: ATTACKING SOLUTIONS TO COUNTER THE 3 v 3 SITUATION NEAR THE SIDELINE.............96

SESSION FOR THIS TACTICAL SITUATION (4 Practices)

1. Quick Combination to Switch Play to the Full Backs in Available Space (Technical Practice) 97

2. Attacking Solutions to Counter the 3 v 3 Situation Near the Sideline in a Zonal Game (Against 2 Forwards) ...98

3. Attacking Solutions to Counter the 3 v 3 Situation Near the Sideline in a Zonal Game (Against 1 Forward) 99

4. Attacking Solutions to Counter the 3 v 3 Situation Near the Sideline in an 11 v 11 Zonal Game 100

CHAPTER 6: CREATING AND EXPLOITING SPACE IN A 4 v 3 (OR 4 v 4) SITUATION AROUND THE BALL AREA 101

Creating and Exploiting Space in a 4 v 3 (or 4 v 4) Situation Around the Ball Area 102

SESSION 8: CREATING AND EXPLOITING SPACE IN A 4 v 3 (OR 4 v 4) SITUATION AROUND THE BALL 104

SESSION FOR THIS TACTICAL SITUATION (4 Practices)

1. Creating and Exploiting Space in Behind in a Technical Practice 105

2. Creating and Exploiting Space Within a 4 v 3 or 4 v 4 Situation in a Dynamic Zonal Practice................. 106

3. Creating and Exploiting Space Within a 4 v 3 or 4 v 4 Situation Near the Sideline in a Zonal Game.......... 108

4. Creating and Exploiting Space Within a 4 v 3 or 4 v 4 Situation Near the Sideline in an 11 v 11 Game........ 110

CHAPTER 7: BUILDING UP PLAY AGAINST ULTRA-OFFENSIVE PRESSING................ 111

Building Up Play Against Ultra-Offensive Pressing... 112

SESSION 9: BUILDING UP PLAY AGAINST ULTRA-OFFENSIVE PRESSING 116

SESSION FOR THIS TACTICAL SITUATION (3 Practices)

1. Quick Combination Play to Break Through Ultra-Offensive Pressing & Receive in Behind an Opponent 117

2. Breaking Through Ultra-Offensive Pressing On One Side of the Pitch in an 8 (+GK) v 8 Game 118

3. Breaking Through Ultra-Offensive Pressing in an 11 v 11 Zonal Game 120

MEET THE AUTHOR

- UEFA 'A' Coaching licence
- M.S.C. in coaching and conditioning

I played for several teams in the Greek professional leagues. At the age of 29 I stopped playing and focused on studying football coaching. I have been head coach of several semi-pro football teams in Greece and worked as a technical director in the Academies of DOXA Dramas (Greek football league, 2nd division).

I wrote and published two books "4-3-3 the application of the system" and "4-4-2 with diamond in midfield, the application of the system" in Greek language. I then decided to proceed in something more specific so coaches would have an idea of how top teams apply the same systems. I published further books with SoccerTutor.com Ltd which have become extremely successful and sold thousands worldwide:

- *FC Barcelona: A Tactical Analysis*
- *Jose Mourinho's Real Madrid: A Tactical Analysis*
- *FC Barcelona Training Sessions*
- *Jürgen Klopp's Attacking and Defending Tactics*
- *Coaching the Juventus 3-5-2*

I have also been invited as an instructor to many coaching seminars and workshops around the world.

This book has been created after studying the playing philosophy of Marcelo Bielsa, and in particular, his Marseille and Athletic Bilbao teams. The aim of the book is to use the innovative tactics of Bielsa to provide a complete guide of how to build up play effectively against high pressing teams. The focus is on building up play from the goalkeeper and expansive football. This style has not only been successful for Bielsa, but has inspired many top coaches such as Pep Guardiola, Mauricio Pochettino, Gerard Martino and Jorge Sampaoli. Bielsa's legacy runs deep in football.

The book includes general tactics (playing philosophy) and specific tactical situations such as:

- *Playing through pressure on the strong side and switching play*
- *Creating and exploiting 3 v 2 situations near the sideline*
- *Building up play against ultra-offensive pressing*

These practices are used to break through the defensive organisation of teams which defend with 1 or 2 forwards (we use the 4-4-2 and 4-2-3-1 as examples) and apply high pressing to disturb the build-up play.

Each chapter has extensive analysis for the tactical situation based on Marcelo Bielsa's tactics and is then followed by a full session to help all coaches adapt the tactics into training sessions for their team.

Athanasios Terzis

MARCELO BIELSA COACH PROFILE

MARCELO BIELSA

Coaching Roles

- Lille OSC Head Coach (2017 - Present)
- Marseille Head Coach (2014 - 2015)
- Athletic Bilbao Head Coach (2011 - 2013)
- Chile National Team Head Coach (2007 - 2010)
- Argentina National Team Head Coach (1998 - 2005)
- Vélez Sársfield (Argentina) Head Coach (1997 - 1998)
- América (Mexico) Head Coach (1995 - 1996)
- Atlas (Mexico) Head Coach (1993 - 1995)
- Newell's Old Boys (Argentina) Head Coach (1990 - 1993)

Honours

- Argentine Primera División (1991, 1992 & 1998)
- Summer Olympics Tournament Gold Medal (2004)
- Copa América Runner-up (2004)
- UEFA Europa League Runner-up (2012)
- Copa Del Rey Runner-up (2012)
- Copa Libertadores Runner-up (1992)

Marcelo Bielsa played for his hometown football team Newell's Old Boys in the Argentine Primera División. His playing career ended at the age of 25 in 1980, at which time he decided to dedicate himself to coaching. He worked at Newell's Old Boys as a scout and as Assistant Coach, until being appointed Head Coach in 1990. He was admired so much for his time at the club, they have since named their stadium after him - 'Estadio Marcelo Bielsa'.

Before leaving Newell's Old Boys in 1993, Bielsa won 2 league titles and got to the final of the Copa Libertadores (1992), losing the final on penalties against Brazilian team São Paulo. He then had spells in Mexico and back in Argentina with Vélez Sársfield, before managing the Argentine national team.

Bielsa's time at Argentina was successful and he was much admired for his style of play. In 2004, they won the Summer Olympics Tournament Gold Medal and were runners up in the Copa América.

He then went on to enjoy further success at international level with Chile, successfully qualifying for the 2010 World Cup in South Africa, qualifying through the group stages and losing to Brazil in the last 16 stage. During his time managing at International level, with Argentina and Chile, is when the football world really woke up to Bielsa's tactical innovations and exciting brand of attacking football.

After his time with Chile, Marcelo Bielsa returned to club football, with Spanish team Athletic Bilbao. In his first season in charge, he led Bilbao to the final of the UEFA Europa League and to the final of the Copa Del Rey. After his time in Spain, Bielsa took over at Marseille where he was commended heavily for his team's style of play and finished fourth in Ligue 1 (France) - he left after one season when many top players were sold against his wishes.

He is now due to take charge of Lille OSC in France, where he will continue to excite with his expansive, attacking style of football - always building up play from the back.

MARCELO BIELSA'S INFLUENCE ON TOP COACHES

Mauricio Pochettino

" He is one of the best managers in the world. "

" There is no doubt that he had an effect on me. He helped me to mature when I was starting my career at Newell's, he helped me in the national team, and he's continued to help me in my coaching career. "

Jorge Sampaoli

" We're followers of Bielsa and of the way he plays the game, but comparisons are unfair, because we're talking about one of the best. "

" People always think that by hiring one of us, they're getting a Bielsa clone, but Marcelo is one of a kind. "

Gerardo Martino

" I've always been a fan of Bielsa, who was just starting out as a coach as my playing career was drawing to a close. "

" Straight away I warmed to his personality and I take great pride in being compared to him. "

Pep Guardiola

" My admiration for Marcelo Bielsa is huge because he makes the players much, much better. "

" Still, I didn't meet one guy, a former player from Marcelo Biesla who speaks badly about him. They are grateful for his influence on their careers in football. "

" He helped me a lot with his advice. Whenever I speak with him, I always feel like he wants to help me. "

" It is important for me to say this about Marcelo because it doesn't matter how many titles he had in his career. We are judged by that – how much success we have, how many titles we have won. But that is much less influential than how he has influenced football and his football players. "

" That is why, for me, he is the best coach in the world. I am looking forward to seeing him in Lille next season. I am pretty sure his influence on their team, their club and their players will be huge – amazing. "

Famous Marcelo Bielsa Quotes

" A man with new ideas is a madman, until his ideas triumph. "

" Conceptually, for me, all the matches are the same - you have to dominate and play everything you can. Anything else does not fit into my ideas. "

" There is no excuse for not going out to win. I feel obliged to do it in every game. "

" Attacking football is the simplest way to victory and success, which is why we play open attacking football. "

" I always tell the boys that football for us is movement, displacement, that we must always be running. "

MARCELO BIELSA'S TACTICS

The Innovative 3-3-3-1 Formation to Build Up Play from the Back

Marcelo Bielsa has mainly used the 4-2-3-1 formation, however his teams can adapt their formation depending on which phase or situation they are in. For building up play from the back, Bielsa uses his trademark system and chooses to shift his teams into a 3-3-3-1 formation (especially when playing against two forwards). He uses this formation as it is very attack minded and he believes it is the best way to break through the opponent's pressure.

Bielsa has used this 3-3-3-1 formation with *Argentina*, *Chile*, *Athletic Bilbao* and *Marseille*. When the midfield is more congested (often against teams that play with one forward and a deep No.10), his teams will adapt to a more defensive minded 3-4-3 formation, so they have an extra player in central midfield to build up play.

Marseille's 3-3-3-1 Formation to Build Up Play from the Back Against 2 Forwards (adapt from 4-2-3-1)

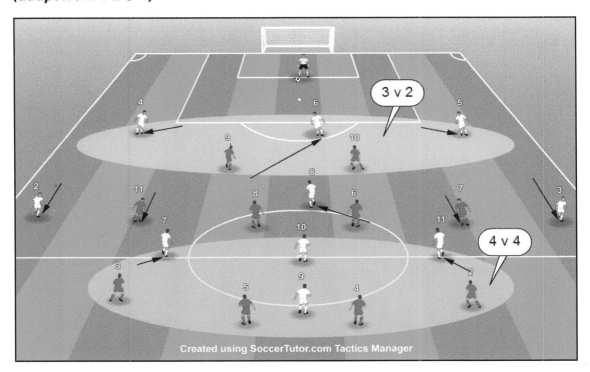

Created using SoccerTutor.com Tactics Manager

This 3-3-3-1 formation allows Marcelo Bielsa's teams to create numerical advantages at the back (3 v 2) and near the sidelines (3 v 2), with a numerical equality (4 v 4) in attack.

One of the central midfielders (6) drops back into the middle of what becomes a back three. Both centre backs (4 & 5) push out wide to potentially receive from the goalkeeper and the full backs push forward in line with the other central midfielder (8).

Marcelo Bielsa Looks for the Following from his Players to Build Up Play:

Goalkeeper: Needs to have a good technical level to receive and play out from the back with accurate passing. Must always be available at a good passing angle for an option back.

Central Midfielders: Stay near to the ball area and provide a passing option to the player in possession. Good technique to play first touch passes as a 'link player' or switch the play with accurate long passing.

Centre Backs: Marcelo Bielsa likes these players to have a high technical level so they are able to receive and pass along the floor from the back, to break through pressure.

Attacking Midfielders: Must always look to move into available passing lanes and act as a 'link player.'

Full Backs: Move forward and take up advanced positions. They are vital for Bielsa's tactics to build up play from the back as they are often the free player and take part in many attacks.

Forward: When the team are building up, the forward should shift across to the strong side (numerical advantage) so that space in behind can be exploited if they break through pressure.

Marcelo Bielsa's Coaching Style

This 3-3-3-1 formation allows the team to create numerical advantages in specific areas of the pitch to break through pressure and then create favourable situations in attack i.e. 4 v 3, 4 v 4, 5 v 4 etc. The key to Bielsa's tactics is the movement, rotations and quick combination play. The players must work hard to move the ball to the free player and create available passing lanes to play forward. At times when Bielsa has not had defenders with a high technical level at his disposal, he has used midfield players in defence to make sure that his team is fully capable of playing out from the back under pressure.

Marcelo Bielsa's unique tactics and attractive style of play have affected football far beyond his own personal successes. He has taught and influenced players and coaches that he has worked with (and not worked with) and they have then implemented elements of his coaching style into the training of their teams. These include Pep Guardiola (Barcelona, Bayern Munich & Manchester City), Mauricio Pochettino (Espanyol, Southampton & Tottenham Hotspur), Gerardo Martino (Barcelona & Argentina) and Jorge Sampaoli (Chile & Sevilla).

Marcelo Bielsa is a student of the game and is well known to analyse hours and hours of games to decipher any new tactical concepts. He is said to have no equal in his work and tactical knowledge - this is what keeps him progressive, as he believes the game is always changing and tactics/style of play can always be improved. He creates videos for individual players and has long discussions with each of them to explain their exact roles and responsibilities they have in all different tactical situations. For building up play, Bielsa focuses on creating space, dragging opponents away and timing movements to receive or act as a link player.

This work is then applied on the training pitch, as each combination and pattern is worked on repeatedly. Each pass and movement is choreographed within a set phase and done over and over again, until Bielsa's players are able to perfect it. This is why, when you watch his teams (analysis shown later in the book), the same patterns are observed and you can see the method being actualised. For this book, these patterns/phases have been recorded and presented in detail - we then provide full sessions so that you can train your team in the same way to build up play against high pressing teams.

MARCELO BIELSA'S ATTACKING PHILOSOPHY

Marcelo Bielsa is famous for his playing philosophy which is based on building up from the back, even when playing against a team which presses high up the pitch.

For a team to be a successful by building up play from the goalkeeper, skilful defenders are needed. At times when Bielsa has not had defenders with a high technical level at his disposal, he has used midfield players in defence to make sure that his team is fully capable of playing out from the back under pressure.

Marcelo Bielsa's Attacking Philosophy

Marcelo Bielsa's playing philosophy includes the following:

- A mix of short and long passing.
- Moving the ball to the free player through 'link players'.
- Attempts to drag opposition players out of position.
- Attempts to stretch the opponent's lines either vertically or horizontally and exploit the gaps created.

Marcelo Bielsa's First Aim

When building up from the back, Marcelo Bielsa's first aim is to provide an available passing option to the goalkeeper. In order for this to be achieved against a high pressing team with 2 forwards, the formation of his team is changed from a 4-2-3-1 to a 3-3-3-1 (attacking option) or the 3-4-3 (more defensive option).

When building up play against teams with 1 forward, Bielsa opts to stick with the 4-2-3-1 formation, but one central midfielder will often drop back if the team wants to switch the play.

Marcelo Bielsa's Second Aim

The second aim is related to the opposition's defensive positioning:

- If the ball is moved near the sidelines, Bielsa's teams attempt to create and exploit a 3 v 2 numerical advantage on that side.
- If the ball is forced towards the centre, through passes are played to players trying to receive between the lines or into the available space which has been created.

Strategies for how to deal with the quick shifting of the opponents towards the sideline, how to counter the attempt of the opposition to create a 3 v 3 situation near the sideline and how to build up against ultra-offensive pressing are also explained within this book.

There are 6 main topics (7 full training sessions) in this book which are all based on Marcelo Bielsa's tactics:

- **Chapter 1:** Building Up Play from the Back Against 2 Forwards
- **Chapter 2:** Building Up Play from the Back Against 1 Forward
- **Chapter 3:** Creating and Exploiting 3 v 2 Situations Near the Sideline
- **Chapter 4:** Attacking Solutions with a 3 v 3 Situation Near the Sideline
- **Chapter 5:** Creating and Exploiting Space in a 4 v 3 (or 4 v 4) Situation Around the Ball Area
- **Chapter 6:** Building Up Play Against Ultra-Offensive Pressing

BUILDING UP PLAY AGAINST HIGH PRESSING TEAMS

BUILDING UP PLAY AGAINST HIGH PRESSING TEAMS

Firstly, I believe the attacking phase is whenever your team is in possession of the ball, even if it is with your goalkeeper. When the defending team's aim is to win possession as high as possible, then they would probably use high pressing. If the attacking team's aim is to use a possession based style of play, they would probably build up play from the goalkeeper (building up play from the back).

What is Building Up Play from the Back?

Building up play from the back is the attempt of the team in possession to move the ball from the goalkeeper to a player in an advanced position, who has available time and space to play a successful forward pass, with a good chance of creating a goal scoring opportunity.

During the last decade, the available time and space for teams in the attacking phase has been significantly restricted. This forced coaches to train their players under conditions of limited space and time in order to adapt to game situations. The players' technique has improved significantly as they have become used to this kind of pressure. This means that players are getting better and better at successfully playing in tight spaces.

Furthermore, during this period, football tactics have also been developed. Coaches have borrowed tactical elements from basketball and tried to apply them on the football pitch - such as finding the free player when a numerical advantage is achieved in a certain part of the pitch. As a result of this, many coaches in the modern game decide to start the attacking phase by building up play from the back.

Attacking Against 1 or 2 Forwards

For this book we have the defensive team using the 4-4-2 (2 forwards) and the 4-2-3-1 (1 forward). This is because they are two of the most popular formations used by coaches during the last decade.

The two formations have many similarities when they are used during the defensive phase. There are four defenders and four midfielders in both formations who move and act in a very similar way. The main difference is the positioning of the No.10 which enables the 4-2-3-1 to have one extra player in midfield, compared with the 4-4-2. This fact differentiates the way the defensive play is carried out by the No.9 and the No.10 within the space in front of the four midfielders.

Teams that play with 2 forwards (4-4-2) during the defensive phase can be very effective when the aim of the team is to apply high pressing, but they obviously lose one player in midfield compared to the 4-2-3-1, which makes it a less solid formation in this area and can make it easier for the attacking team to receive passes in between the forward and midfield lines.

Defending with 1 forward (4-2-3-1) may not be as effective when applying high pressing, but it certainly makes it more difficult for the opposition to make and receive passes in between the forward and midfield lines (especially from the sides towards the centre). This is due to the presence of the No.10 within this space who can block the passes and prevent attempts of the opponents to switch play.

It must be mentioned that there are some teams that use the 4-2-3-1 formation and carry out the defensive in front of the four midfielders with tactics closer to that of the 4-4-2. A good example of this is Jürgen Klopp at Borussia Dortmund and Liverpool.

REQUIREMENTS FOR BUILDING UP PLAY FROM THE BACK

Accurate Passing by the Goalkeeper

This element is necessary in order to move the ball from the goalkeeper to the target player if he is free to receive in space. A skilful goalkeeper is a must to avoid giving away possession in dangerous areas of the pitch.

Good Technique for Running with the Ball (Ball Control)

The aim is to move the ball forward quickly and create a numerical advantage in specific areas of the pitch. A defender or midfielder who is technically skilled in moving with the ball ensures safety, and makes sure we avoid needlessly losing possession in our own half.

Accurate Forward Passing

Accurate passing is needed to make a successful forward pass and take advantage of a numerical advantage, which is created in a specific area of the pitch. If an inaccurate pass is played when the team has a numerical advantage, the collective effort will be of no use, as possession will be lost when we have a favourable situation and a good chance to attack.

The Four Required Steps

To successfully build up from the back, the team in possession has to follow four steps.

- **Step 1:** Providing a free passing option for the goalkeeper
- **Step 2:** Moving the ball to the target or free player
- **Step 3:** Creating a numerical advantage in specific areas of the pitch
- **Step 4:** Take advantage (exploit) the numerical advantage

COACHING FORMAT

1. TACTICAL SITUATION AND ANALYSIS

- The analysis is based on recurring patterns of play observed within **Marcelo Bielsa's Olympique Marseille** and **Athletic Bilbao** teams. Once the same phase of play occurred a number of times (at least 10) the tactics would be seen as a pattern.

- Each action, pass, individual movement (with or without the ball) and the positioning of each player on the pitch including their body shape, are presented with a full description.

2. FULL TRAINING SESSION FROM THE TACTICAL SITUATION

- Technical and Functional Unopposed Practices
- Tactical Opposed Practices
- Objective and Full Description
- Restrictions, Progressions, Variations & Coaching Points (if applicable)

KEY

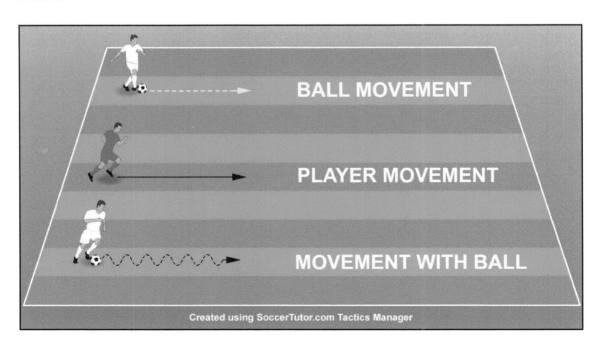

BALL MOVEMENT

PLAYER MOVEMENT

MOVEMENT WITH BALL

Created using SoccerTutor.com Tactics Manager

16

CHAPTER 1

BUILDING UP PLAY FROM THE BACK AGAINST 2 FORWARDS

POSITIONING TO BUILD UP PLAY AGAINST 2 FORWARDS

Within Marcelo Bielsa's 4-2-3-1 formation, the players aim to build up play from the back. The basic formation is shown in the diagram below. Normally the centre backs (4 & 5) take up wide positions, while the full backs (2 & 3) move into advanced positions.

Positioning with the 4-2-3-1 Formation Against 2 Forwards

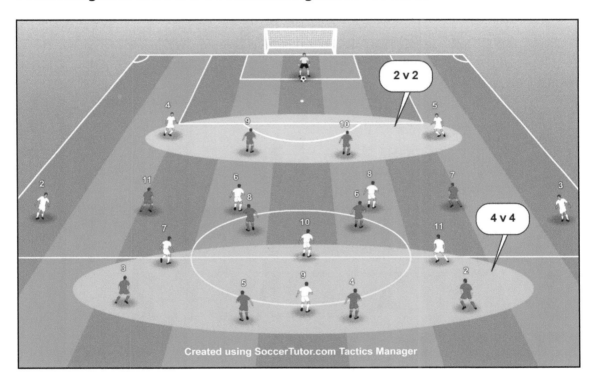

This basic formation set-up does not work well when matched up against a defending team which plays with 2 forwards. There is a 2 v 2 situation at the back which makes it hard to play the ball out from the goalkeeper. This is why Bielsa changes this initial formation to build up play from the back.

These changes are fully outlined in the following pages, as we show how Marcelo Bielsa adapts his formation to best build up play from the back when playing against a team with 2 forwards.

ASSESSMENT:

There are some opposition teams that use the 4-2-3-1 formation and create this same situation by pushing the No.10 high up the pitch (e.g. Klopp's Dortmund and Liverpool teams). This means that there is still a 2 v 2 situation at the back for the team and they must find a solution.

STEP 1: PROVIDING A FREE PASSING OPTION FOR THE GOALKEEPER AGAINST 2 FORWARDS

2 v 2 at the Back Against 2 Forwards

When the defending team plays with 2 forwards, there is a 2 v 2 situation at the back which makes the direct pass from the goalkeeper to one of the centre backs a risky choice.

In order to play out safely from the goalkeeper, he should be given the option to pass the ball to a free player.

3 v 2 at the Back Against 2 Forwards

To make sure that the goalkeeper can play the ball out safely to a free player, Marcelo Bielsa makes sure to create a numerical advantage at the back with 3 players against the 2 opposing forwards.

This can be obtained through several tactical adjustments which will be explained on the following pages.

1a) Creating a 3 v 2 Situation at the Back by Adapting to an Attacking 3-3-3-1 Formation

When building up play against teams that play with 1 forward, no further action has to be taken at the back as there is already a numerical advantage (2 v 1). However, when playing against 2 forwards, tactical adjustments have to be made.

The diagram below shows the attacking movements used by Marcelo Bielsa to build up from the back. Other top coaches, such as Pep Guardiola have also used this tactic. When starting in a 4-2-3-1 formation, the role of dropping back is normally carried out by the deepest central midfielder- the 'holding midfielder'. The midfielder who drops back between the centre backs should possess good passing skills and good control of the ball, just like Sergio Busquets or Xabi Alonso.

Adapting the 4-2-3-1 to 3-3-3-1 When Building Up Play Against 2 Forwards: The Central Midfielder Drops Back Between the 2 Centre Backs

Marcelo Bielsa most often sets his team up in a 4-2-3-1 formation, but after a central midfielder (No.6) drops back into defence and the full backs push forward, the formation changes to 3-3-3-1. This is an attack-minded formation as there are 4 players in advanced positions, creating a 4 v 4 situation in the attacking line. This equality in numbers is always in favour of the attacking team. The fact that the 3-3-3-1 creates advantages for the attacking team means that Marcelo Bielsa sometimes use the 3-3-3-1 as a permanent formation, and not only when building up play from the back.

Adapting the 4-3-2-1 to 3-3-2-2 When Building Up Play Against 2 Forwards: The Central Midfielder Drops Back Towards the Sideline

If the 4-2-3-1 formation is used by the attacking team, a numerical advantage with 3 v 2 at the back can also be created with one of the 2 central midfielders dropping deeper and towards the sideline (see No.6's movement in the diagram above).

The centre backs (4 & 5) move across and the other central midfielder (8) moves into a central position.

In the diagram example the attacking team adapt the 4-3-2-1 formation to the 3-3-3-2, to build up play from the goalkeeper.

1b) Creating a 3 v 2 Situation at the Back by Adapting to a More Defensive 3-4-3 Formation

The tactical adjustments on the previous two pages are attack-minded, as a 4 v 4 situation is created in the attacking line. However, there is another option to create a numerical advantage at the back which Marcelo Bielsa uses with his teams. The team retain more safety in midfield but it is more defence-minded, as the match up in the attacking line changes to 3 v 4 in favour of the defending team (see diagram below).

Adapting the 4-2-3-1 to 3-4-3 When Building Up Play Against 2 Forwards

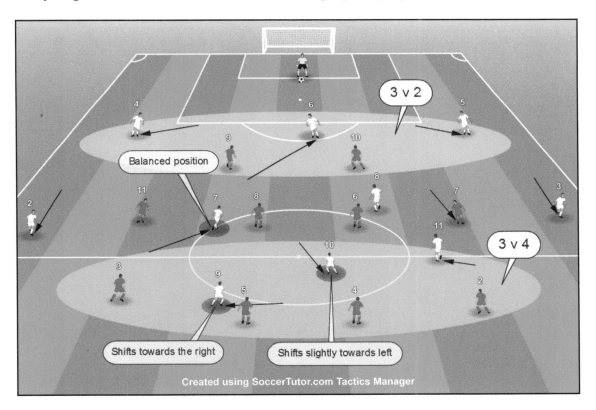

In this situation, the team adapt their 4-2-3-1 formation again. The central midfielder (6) drops between the centre backs and one of the wingers (No.7 in diagram) drops back into central midfield to retain balance and create a line of 4 midfielders.

The winger who drops back (7) is ready to play as a central midfielder, and if the ball is moved forward, he can then join the three advanced players to attack.

The forward (9) shifts towards the right and the No.10 shifts slightly towards the left to keep the formation, which now has the form of 3-4-3 and is more balanced.

There is a 3 v 2 advantage at the back to build up play, but now there is a 3 v 4 disadvantage in attack.

STEP 2: MOVING THE BALL TO THE TARGET OR FREE PLAYER AGAINST 2 FORWARDS

After completing the first step (providing a free passing option for the goalkeeper), the next aim for Marcelo Bielsa is for his players at the back to take advantage of the numerical advantage and move the ball to the spare player. This player will probably have available time and space on the ball and if he manages to overcome the pressure of the forward(s), the team will have many possibilities to create a numerical advantage in specific areas of the pitch. The ideal situation is the one in which the ball is directed to the 'target player' (see below).

2a) Who is the Target Player?

Creating a 3 v 2 Numerical Advantage Near the Sidelines with Bielsa's 3-3-3-1 Formation Against 2 Forwards (Attacking Option)

When Marcelo Bielsa adapts his 4-2-3-1 formation to the 3-3-3-1 for the attacking phase against 2 forwards, they have a 3 v 2 numerical advantage at the back and a 3 v 2 advantage near both sidelines. The 2 centre backs who pull out wide are both 'target players'. These numerical advantages are created because the 3-3-3-1 is an attack-minded formation.

ASSESSMENT:

1. In order for this numerical advantage to be exploited, the 'target player' must receive the ball having overcome the pressure of the forward nearest to him. If the opposing forward manages to close the 'target player' down, the defending team (blues) will manage to retain balance as equality in numbers will be created near the sideline.

2. The defensive option of adapting the 4-2-3-1 formation to a 3-4-3 for building up play does not create this numerical advantage (3 v 2) on both sides - see next page.

Creating a 3 v 2 Numerical Advantage Near the Sidelines with Bielsa's 3-4-3 Formation Against 2 Forwards (Defensive Option)

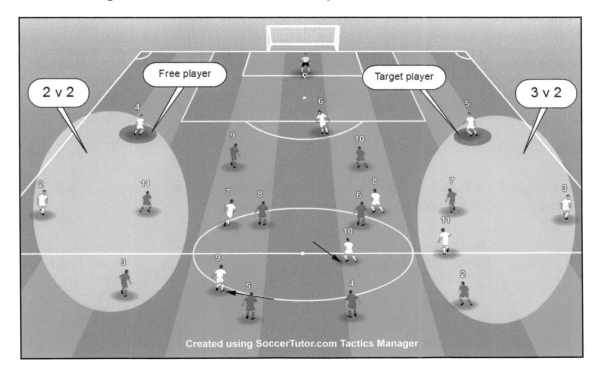

For the defensive option of adapting the 4-2-3-1 to a 3-4-3 formation to build up play from the back, a 3 v 2 situation is created on one side (left) but not on the other side (right) where there is a 2 v 2. This means that the left centre back (5) is the 'target player' and if he can receive and overcome the pressure of blue No.10, there is a strong possibility for the team to exploit the 3 v 2 numerical advantage on that side. Alternatively, if both No.5 and No.6 are marked and cannot receive, the ball must be moved to No.4 as he will be the 'free player'. In this situation there is no numerical advantage near the sideline, as it will be 2 v 2.

ASSESSMENT:

1. It is very likely that the 'target player' is changed during the build-up, as the quick shifting of the opposition players may affect the situation in different areas of the pitch. If the 'free player' is positioned on the weak side, the ball must still be moved towards him.

2. In cases when the ball is moved to the 'free player' instead of the 'target player', there is still a possibility for the attacking team to create a numerical advantage with some tactical adjustments (see example shown on next page).

Changing the 2 v 2 Situation Near the Sideline to 3 v 2 with the Forward Shifting Across After 'Free Player' Receives (Bielsa's 3-4-3)

No.9's shift changes the situation from 2 v 2 to 3 v 2

Created using SoccerTutor.com Tactics Manager

As both No.6 and No.5 ('target player') are marked by the 2 blue forwards (No.9 and No.10 respectively), the right centre back (4) stays free of marking and becomes the 'free player' (not the 'target player').

When No.4 receives the ball from the goalkeeper, there is initially a 2 v 2 situation near the sideline. In these situations, Bielsa's teams are able to make tactical adjustments to create a numerical advantage.

The forward (9) shifts towards the strong side, while No.10 moves into the forward's position. A 3 v 2 numerical advantage is now created on the strong side, as shown in the diagram.

2b) Moving the Ball to the Target Player or Free Player

Building Up Play Against 2 Forwards When Both 'Target Players' are Marked (Bielsa's Attacking 3-3-3-1 Formation)

Both target players (4 & 5) marked, so No.6 receives in the centre

Moving the ball to the 'target player' can be achieved in two different ways:

1. If the 'target player' is free of marking because the two opposition forwards are focused on the other two players, the ball can be moved to the 'target player' with a direct pass.

2. If the 'target player' or 'target players' are marked, the goalkeeper passes short to No.6 who is the 'free player'. The ball can then be directed to a 'target player' via a 'link player' (see diagram on next page).

Using a 'Link Player' to Move the Ball to the 'Target Player'

Created using SoccerTutor.com Tactics Manager

This follows on from the diagram on the previous page. As soon as No.6 receives, blue No.10 moves to apply pressure and block the pass towards No.5 (who is now free of marking) at the same time.

No.6 passes forward to the central midfielder (8) who is able to act as the 'link player' and pass the ball to No.5, who has moved forward to receive in space.

This kind of combination and movement is key when building up the play from the back against 2 forwards. If the pass to the 'target player' is not possible, the 'free player' can receive and draw pressure, then use a 'link player' to find a 'target player' who is left unmarked.

ASSESSMENT:

1. Moving the ball directly to a 'target player' or through a 'link player' can be applied to all tactical situations and formations.

2. If the defensive option of Bielsa's 4-2-3-1 (3-4-3 as explained before) is used, there are then two midfielders who can play as 'link players'. This may be an advantage if the opposing forwards apply pressure in such a way as to force the play inside, blocking the passing lanes towards the sidelines.

2c) Building Up Play and Attacking from the Centre When the 2 Opposition Forwards Force Play Inside

The central area of the pitch is the most crucial - if a player receives with time and space on the ball in the centre, he will have many options available. A defensively well organised team would usually prevent the opposition from achieving this, however, sometimes teams have a strategy to squeeze the play and force the ball towards the inside. In this situation (shown in diagram below), the 2 opposition forwards stay wide and leave No.6 to receive and move forward with the ball.

Even in this situation, the attacking team should be prepared to break through the pressure.

Finding Passing Lanes and Available Space when Play is Forced Inside

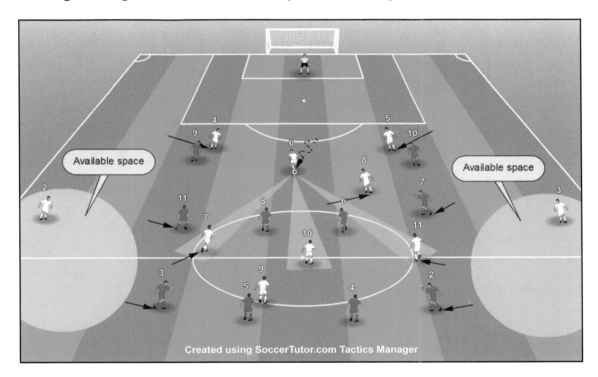

No.6 receives and moves forward as the two blue forwards (9 & 10) stay wide. The three passing options for the player in possession (6) are the through passes towards the midfielders between the lines (7, 10 or 11), which could lead to them receiving and turning to attack in the opposition's half.

Alternatively, as the blue team's wingers (7 & 11) converge to narrow the passing lanes, more space is available for the wing backs (2 & 3) near the sidelines. The more the blue team's wingers converge to block the passing lanes, the passes towards the No.7 and No.11 become almost impossible, but the space near the sidelines becomes bigger for an easy aerial pass into the available space.

Playing a Through Pass in the Centre When the Opposition Wingers Stay Wide

This is an alternative situation to the previous diagram.

If the opposition wingers (7 & 11) stay wide to restrict the space near the sidelines (rather than converge into the centre), the passing lanes get wider and a through pass is made much easier.

In the diagram example, No.6 is able to play a through pass to No.7 who turns. This takes all 4 opposition midfielders out of the game.

It is possible to create a 6 v 4 situation for the attack if the wing backs are in advanced positions.

Opposition Full Back Moves Forward to Stop Midfielder Receiving Between the Lines, but Space is then Created in Behind

AVAILABLE
SPACE BEHIND
FULL BACK

Moves forward to prevent No.7
from receiving and turning

Created using SoccerTutor.com Tactics Manager

In this variation of the previous diagram, the opposition's left back (3) moves forward to mark No.7 and prevent him from receiving and turning.

Although this blocks off No.7 as a good passing option, the left back's movement forward creates space behind him.

The right wing back (2) makes a run forward to receive the aerial pass in the available space.

In this situation we could have a 5 v 4 situation for the attack.

Opposition Wingers Move Inside to Make Compact Midfield Which Creates Space Near the Sideline for a 2 v 1

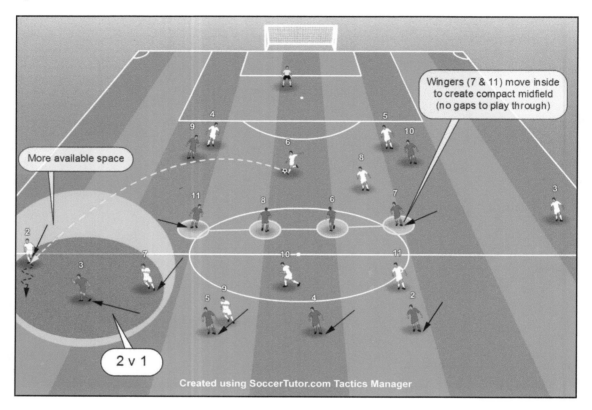

If the opposition's midfielders retain a straight line and converge towards the centre with short distances between each other, more space is available near the sidelines.

This often creates a 2 v 1 situation near the sideline and can be exploited by the attacking team.

In the diagram example, the right wing back (2) receives and is closed down by the blue left back (3). No.7 moves across to create a 2 v 1 situation they can exploit.

We have a 5 v 4 situation for the attack again.

Opposition's Full Back & Winger Work Together to Cover our Winger and Wing Back, so the Ball is Passed Inside to the No.10

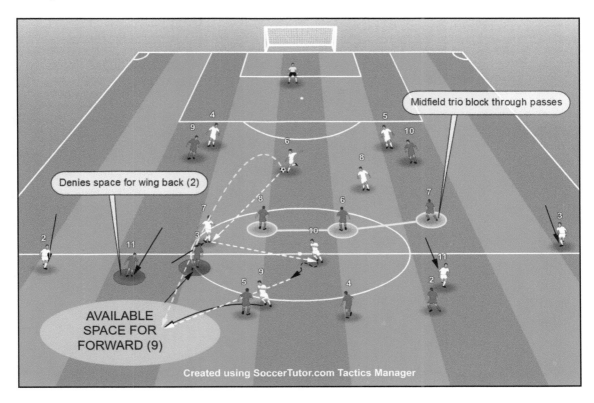

Created using SoccerTutor.com Tactics Manager

If the blue winger (11) follows the white wing back (2) and the blue left back (3) pushes forward to prevent No.7 from receiving and turning, space is still created behind the blue left back (3).

The difference this time is which player can exploit the space created. The wing back (2) is now covered, so the forward (9) makes a run into the space.

The ball can be passed directly into the space for the forward to run onto (yellow line) or after a passing combination (white lines).

ASSESSMENT:

1. It is very important that the opposing midfielders are not able to intercept a bad pass from No.6, as it is then possible that the team would have to defend a 2 v 2 attack.
2. The defensive tactics detailed above (blue opposition team) can only be used with formations that have 2 forwards, like the 4-4-2 (and Klopp's 4-2-3-1 when the No.10 is in an advanced position.

SESSION 1

Based on Tactics of Marcelo Bielsa

Building Up Play and Attacking from the Centre

SESSION FOR THIS TACTICAL SITUATION (3 PRACTICES)
1. Reading the Tactical Situation to Play the Right Pass When Building Up Play from the Centre

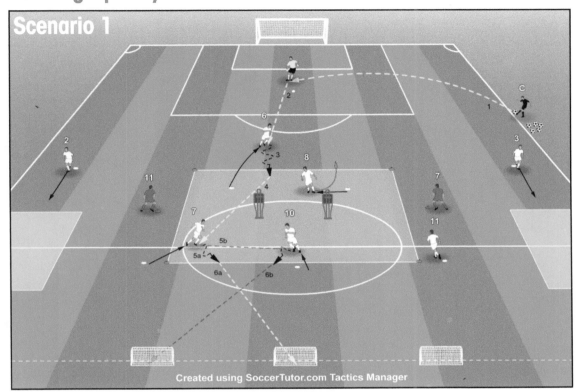

Scenario 1

Created using SoccerTutor.com Tactics Manager

Objective: Practice building up play and attacking from the centre (you can adapt this to different formations).

Description

Using 2/3 of a full pitch, we mark out 1 central area, 2 side areas, 2 blue mannequins and 3 mini goals as shown. We have 7 white players (+GK) who all start on the white cones and 2 blue wingers who start on the blue cones.

The practice starts as soon as the goalkeeper receives the long pass from the coach. We are practicing Marcelo Bielsa's tactics, so at this point the white players adjust from their 4-2-3-1 positions to form a 1-3-3 (from the 3-3-3-1 described in the analysis within this chapter).

The central midfielder (6) drops back, receives from the goalkeeper and moves forward. The white midfielders who can be potential receivers (7 & 10) move inside the central area. No.6 has to read the reaction of the blue winger/s and make the best decision.

Scenario 1: If the blue winger stays wide to control the space, the correct choice is a through pass between the winger and a mannequin (representing central midfielders). The white midfielder (No.7 in diagram) can either receive, turn and pass into the mini goal himself or play a first time pass to No.10.

Restriction: The midfielders must receive, turn and pass within the central area.

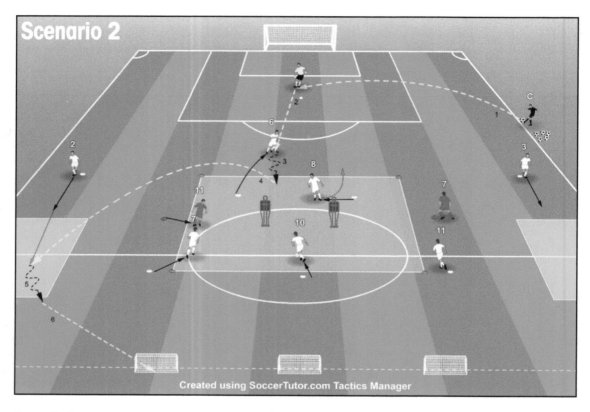

Scenario 2: This second diagram shows the decision making when the blue winger (11) moves inside the central area to create a compact midfield.

Instead of attempting a through pass, No.6 plays an accurate aerial pass for the forward run of the wing back (No.2 in diagram). The wing back then receives and passes into the small goal.

Restriction: The long pass to the wing back must be directed and received within the yellow side area.

Coaching Points
1. Players need to quickly read the tactical situation and demonstrate the correct decision making.
2. There needs to be synchronised movements, good ball reception, turning and combination play within limited space and accurate passing.

2. Reading the Tactical Situation When Building Up Play from the Centre in a Functional Practice

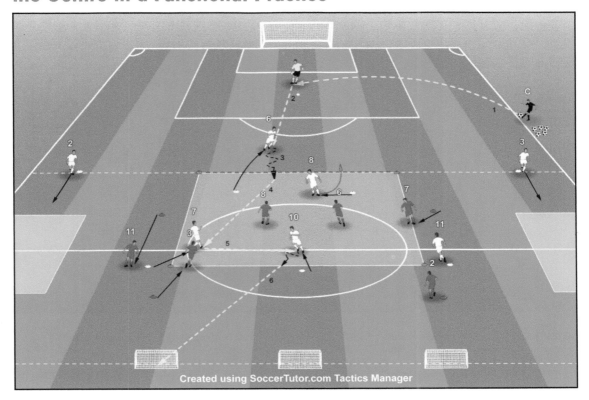

Created using SoccerTutor.com Tactics Manager

Description

This is a progression of the previous practice- we add 2 full backs (2 & 3) and 2 central midfielders (6 & 8) to replace the blue mannequins. The white team have to now overcome pressure from 2 central midfielders and take into account the reaction of the blue full backs, as well as the wingers. The whites try to score in the small goals and if the blues win possession, they try to dribble the ball through the white (1 point) or red line (3 points) within 8-10 seconds.

The following different options are explained fully in the analysis within this chapter on pages 29 to 32:

1. Playing a through pass in the centre when the opposition wingers stay wide - *Page 29*.
2. Opposition full back moves forward to stop midfielder receiving between lines, but space is then created out wide for the full back (who can receive an aerial pass in the space behind the opposition full back). - *Page 30*.
3. Opposition wingers move inside to make compact midfield which creates space near the sideline for a 2 v 1 (the full back can receive an aerial pass within the side area) - *Page 31*.
4. Opposition full back & winger work together to cover our winger and full back, so the ball is passed first time by No.7 (link player), inside to the No.10 - *Page 32 & shown in diagram above*.

Restrictions: The same as the previous practice but a long pass from No.6 behind the blue full back (if he moves forward) can be received outside of the yellow side area.

PROGRESSION

3. Reading the Tactical Situation When Building Up Play from the Centre in a Zonal Game

Created using SoccerTutor.com Tactics Manager

Description

In the final practice of this session, we mark out 5 zones as shown and play an 11 v 11 game. The practice starts with the coach's pass to the goalkeeper and his pass to No.6 in the centre. The white team move from 4-2-3-1 to Bielsa's 3-3-3-1 formation to build up play and the blues use the 4-4-2 formation.

The whites aim to build up play from the centre by reading the tactical situation and making the appropriate decisions - see previous practice for different options. They then try to score a goal past the goalkeeper.

The blues aim is to defend, win the ball and then score themselves (within 8-10 seconds). If a blue player manages to dribble the ball through the white or red line they get an extra 1 or 3 points respectively.

Restrictions

1. The blue players cannot enter the yellow zone when defending.
2. Restrictions concerning the central area are removed but we leave it there as it still helps the white players read the situation e.g. If the blue winger enters the area, then there is probably space near the sideline for the full back.

CHAPTER 2

MOVING THE BALL TO THE TARGET PLAYER ON THE WEAK SIDE

MOVING THE BALL TO THE 'TARGET PLAYER' ON THE WEAK SIDE

In this situation, the 'target player' receives the pass from the goalkeeper, but the opposing forward (9) manages to put him under pressure, so creating a numerical advantage on that side is no longer possible.

3 v 2 Situation is Prevented on the Strong Side, but a 3 v 2 Exists on Weak Side

Created using SoccerTutor.com Tactics Manager

The blue forward (9) closes down the centre back in possession (No.4) and puts him under pressure after the first pass from the goalkeeper. A 3 v 3 or a 4 v 4 situation is created around the ball area, which means that creating a numerical advantage in favour of the attacking team is almost impossible.

A 3 v 2 situation exists on the weak side and the 'target player' is now No.5. These are the two aims:

1. Switch the play to No.5 and take advantage of a 3 v 2 situation near the sideline.

2. Switch the play to No.3 in an advanced position to create a 2 v 1 situation (No.3 and No.11 versus blue No.2).

Option 1: Pass Back to Goalkeeper Who Acts as a 'Link Player' to Switch the Play

Blocks inside pass

3 v 2

Created using SoccerTutor.com Tactics Manager

As explained on the previous page, the attacking team (whites) have a 3 v 3 or 4 v 4 situation around the ball area. The first and simplest option is a back pass to the goalkeeper who acts as 'link player'.

The goalkeeper will then pass to No.5, who can move forward with plenty of space and time.

The closest forward (blue No.10) is too far away to put him under pressure.

A 3 v 2 situation is created near the sideline in favour of the attacking team.

Option 2: If the Pass Back to the Goalkeeper is Blocked, the Inside Pass Will Probably Be Free

In the second option, the central midfielder (8) is used to move the ball to the weak side.

The blue forward (9) blocks the pass back to the goalkeeper. However, No.9's positioning means he is unable to block the inside pass at the same time. This enables the team to use the central midfielder (8) to switch the play to No.5 (target player).

This option can be used against two forwards if the forward away from the ball (No.10) is in a high position and away from the strong side. There also needs to be enough space between the lines for No.8 to receive, turn and pass.

Option 3: Using the Central Midfielder to Switch the Play After Quick Combination Play

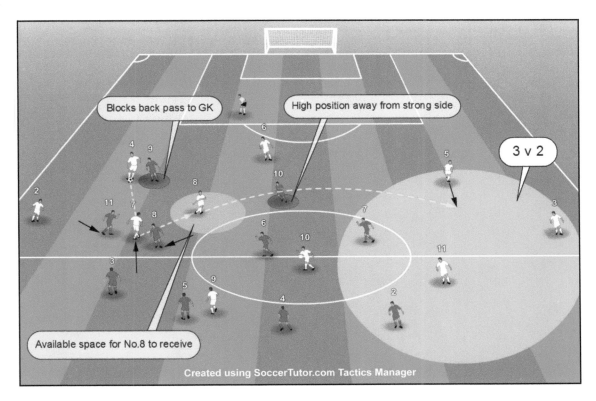

In this variation, No.7 drops back into a deep position between the lines and receives the pass from No.4. This pass draws the two blue players (11 and 8) towards him and out of their positions, as they move to close him down - space is created for No.8 to receive the next pass and then switch the play to No.5 again.

No.8 does not have to turn this time as he can receive facing the opposition's goal and can even switch play with his first touch.

If No.8 is being marked by blue No.10, No.7 can simply pass back to the goalkeeper or No.6.

Option 4: If the Pass Back to GK + Inside Pass Are Blocked, Full Back Acts as a 'Link Player' to Switch Play

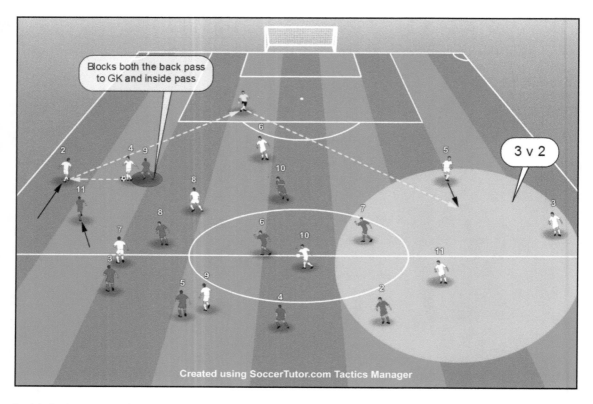

In this final option, the blue forward (9) applies pressure to No.4 in such a way that blocks the pass back to the goalkeeper and the inside pass.

The white wing back (2) reads the tactical situation, so drops back to get free of marking and receive the pass from No.4.

The wing back (2) becomes the 'link player' and passes the ball back to the goalkeeper. From there, the goalkeeper can switch the play to the 'target player' No.5 - the team has a 3 v 2 situation near the sideline again.

SESSION 2

Based on Tactics of Marcelo Bielsa

Playing Through Pressure on the Strong Side and Switching Play Against 2 Forwards

SESSION FOR THIS TACTICAL SITUATION (2 PRACTICES)
1. Pattern of Play to Build Up and Switch the Play Against 2 Forwards

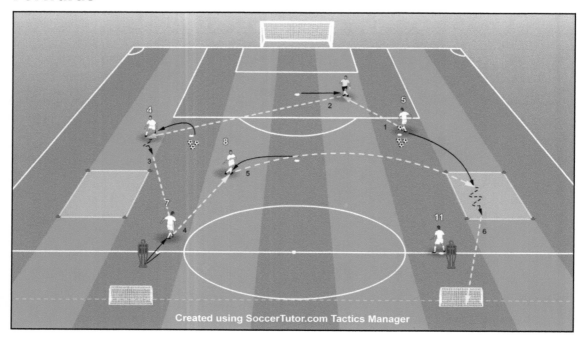

Created using SoccerTutor.com Tactics Manager

Objective: We work on the tactical aspects of playing through pressure on the strong side and switching play. The practice can be adapted to various formations.

Description

Using an area 10 yards longer than half a full pitch, we have a minimum of 5 outfield players - you can have 10 total so there are 2 players at each position. Using Bielsa's building up play tactics against 2 forwards, the players adopt the 2-1-2 formation from the 3-3-3-1. We have 2 centre backs (4 & 5), a central midfielder (8) and 2 attacking midfielders (7 & 11) on the halfway line.

The practice starts with the left centre back (5) who passes to the goalkeeper. The goalkeeper then passes to the right centre back (4) who opens up, receives and plays the next pass forward.

At the same time, the winger (7) gets free of marking and passes first time back to the central midfielder (8) who provides a passing option. As soon as No.8 receives, the centre back on the other side (5) moves forward towards the marked area, receives the long pass within the area and scores in the small goal.

We then perform the same combination starting with No.4's pass to the goalkeeper. The goalkeeper then passes to No.5, who passes to No.11. No.11 passes back to the central midfielder (8), who switches play towards No.4.

Coaching Points

1. Players need to focus on their timing - synchronising movements and approaching the ball on the move.
2. The central midfielder must focus on producing accurate long passes which land inside the side areas.

45

PROGRESSION

2. Playing Through Pressure on the Strong Side Against 2 Forwards and Switching Play in an 8 (+GK) v 6 Game

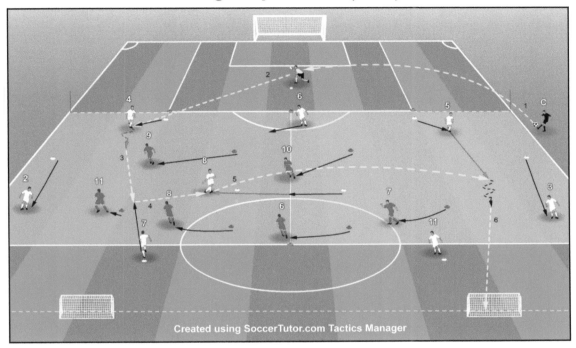

Created using SoccerTutor.com Tactics Manager

Objective: We work on the tactical aspects of playing through pressure on the strong side and switching play.

Description

Using 2/3 of a full pitch, we mark out the area between the halfway line and the penalty area. We have 1 full size goal with a goalkeeper and 2 small goals in the positions shown. The white team adjust their formation to 3-3-2 from Bielsa's 3-3-3-1 to build up play and the blue team are in a 4-2 formation with 2 forwards.

The practice starts with the coach's long pass to the goalkeeper. The white players move from the white cones and readjust their shape to counter the 4-2 formation. The goalkeeper passes to either No.4 or No.5.

The closest forward (No.9 in diagram) applies pressure to prevent a 3 v 2 situation on that side. The rest of the blue players shift towards the strong side (left side of diagram) and they have a numerical equality or advantage around the ball area. Their aim is to prevent the switch of play, win the ball and then score within 8-10 seconds.

The white team aim to play through the pressure with the help of No.7 and switch play towards the other side where they have a 2 v 1 (or 3 v 2) situation. The whites then try to take advantage of this and score.

Restriction

The blue winger on the weak side (No.7 in diagram) does shift across but remains on the weak side.

Coaching Point

The players need to read the tactical situation and make the necessary movements and passes to switch play.

46

SESSION 3

Based on Tactics of Marcelo Bielsa

Switching Play Against 2 Forwards and Exploiting an Advantage on the Weak Side

SESSION FOR THIS TACTICAL SITUATION (4 PRACTICES)
1. Pattern of Play to Build Up and Switch the Play Against 2 Forwards + Attacking Combinations on the Weak Side

Created using SoccerTutor.com Tactics Manager

Description

Using an area 15 yards longer than half a pitch, we mark out 8 mannequins (or large cones) to represent opposition players and 4 areas in wide positions. We have the back four, 3 midfield players, 1 forward and 2 goalkeepers (in full sized goals).

The practice starts with the coach's pass to the goalkeeper, who receives and moves towards one side, before passing to a centre back (No.4 in diagram) who opens up. To switch the play, the centre back has 4 options:

1. Pass back to goalkeeper who acts as a 'link player' to switch play *(see page 40)*.
2. Direct pass to central midfielder (8) who switches play *(see page 41)*.
3. Central midfielder switches play after winger (7) is used as a 'link player' *(see page 42 & both diagrams)*.
4. Full back acts as a 'link player' to switch play via the goalkeeper *(see page 43)*.

Which attacking combination the players then carry out depends on which area the pass is received in. If it is the deepest one *(scenario 1 in diagram above)*, the following happens:

Scenario 1: Centre back (5) receives, moves forward and passes into the other area. The full back moves forward to receive the next pass and No.11 makes a run in behind the mannequin (defender) and into the end zone.

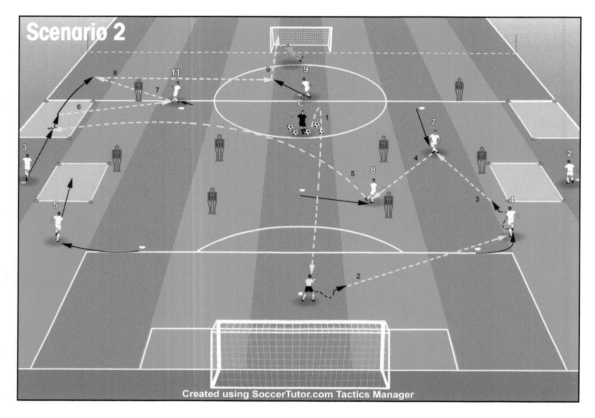

Scenario 2: In this example, the central midfielder (8) switches play into the more advanced area. The full back (3) receives and plays a 1-2 combination with No.11, and receives in behind the mannequin (defender).

Scenario 3: The last scenario is the full back (No.3 in diagram) receiving and No.11 making an overlapping run to receive in behind *(not shown in either diagram).*

The team then try to score past the goalkeeper. The forward (9) times his run to try and finish.

Rules

1. The switch of play must be carried out at speed (within 6-8 seconds from the time the goalkeeper delivers the first pass).
2. The combination play on the weak side must also be finished within 6-8 seconds, from the time the long pass is received.

Coaching Points

1. Players need to focus on their timing - synchronised movements and approaching the ball on the move.
2. The central midfielder (8) must focus on producing accurate long passes.
3. All actions have to be taken at speed.

PROGRESSION

2. Switching Play Against 2 Forwards and Exploiting an Advantage on the Weak Side in a Functional Practice

Objective: We work on playing through pressure, switching the play to the weak side and attacking in a 3 v 2 situation near the sideline.

Description

Using 2/3 of a full pitch, we mark out 4 blue mannequins, 2 side zones and an end zone. The white team have 9 outfield players and the blues have 4 - there are 2 goalkeepers in full sized goals at either end.

The practice starts with the coach's pass to the goalkeeper, who receives and moves towards one side, before passing to a centre back (No.4 in diagram), who opens up. The ball should then be directed into the side zone and the whites use one of the combinations outlined in the previous practice and switch the play to the weak side.

If the centre back receives (No.5 in diagram), the whites have a 3 v 2 advantage in the side zone on the weak side. If the full back receives (No.3 in diagram), they have a 2 v 1 advantage. The aim is to dribble through the red line or receive a pass beyond it, in the end zone.

Scenario 1: In the diagram above, the centre back (5) passes to the full back (3). The winger (11) then makes a diagonal run in behind the blue full back, receives in the end zone and tries to score with help from No.9 & No.10.

|

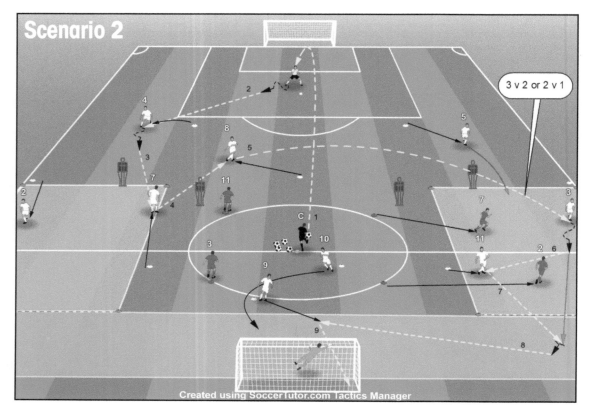

Scenario 2: In scenario 2 (diagram above), the full back (3) receives in a 2 v 1 situation and plays a 1-2 combination with the winger (11), making an overlapping run to receive in behind the blue full back. Once in the end zone, he tries to score with help from No.9 & No.10.

Scenario 3: The full back (No.3 in diagram) receives in a 2 v 1 situation and draws in the defender (blue No.2) - white No.11 makes an overlapping run outside his teammate (full back) to receive a pass in behind *(not shown in either diagram)*.

Restrictions

1. The white team have 6-8 seconds to exploit their numerical advantage in the side zone, from the time that the long pass (switch) is received.
2. The blues are not allowed to defend within the end zone.

Coaching Points

1. The white players have to read the tactical situation and carry out the appropriate combination to exploit the numerical advantage.
2. The exploitation of the numerical advantage should be done quickly and efficiently.

PROGRESSION

3. Switching Play Against 2 Forwards and Exploiting an Advantage on the Weak Side in a Functional Game

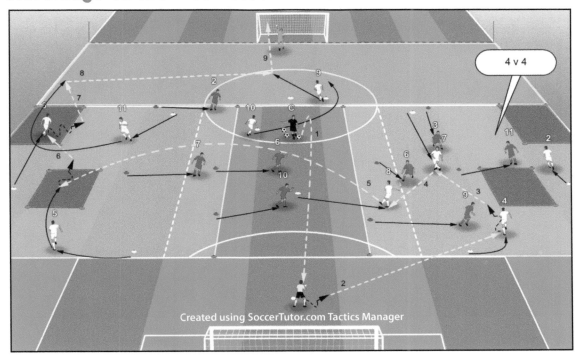

4 v 4

Created using SoccerTutor.com Tactics Manager

Description

In this progression of the previous practice, we now have 9 white outfield players and 8 blue. There are 2 goalkeepers with full sized goals in 18 yard zones. All the players start on their respective cones and then adjust accordingly to the situation.

The practice starts with the coach's pass to the goalkeeper, who receives within a side zone (No.4 in diagram). There is a 4 v 4 situation with the blue forward (9) shifting across. All the other blue players shift across to this side also and the blues aim to win the ball, and then score with a counter attack within 8-10 seconds.

The white team read the tactical situation and either attack on the strong side by dribbling the ball into the end zone or receiving a pass within it, before crossing and scoring - this is if the blues are not organised well. If this is not possible, the white team use the best option described in the previous 2 practices to switch play towards the weak side. The whites can then also use the attacking combinations used in the previous 2 practices after receiving the switch - trying to score with help from No.9 and No.10. Play on both sides.

Restrictions: The blue players don't defend on the weak or inside the end zone, as the focus of this practice is for the whites to overcome pressure on the strong side.

Coaching Points

1. The white players should read the tactical situation and choose the right solution to switch play.
2. The solution should be carried out at speed.

PROGRESSION

4. Switching Play Against 2 Forwards and Exploiting an Advantage on the Weak Side in an 11 v 11 Zonal Game

3 v 2 or 2 v 1 for 6-8 seconds

Created using SoccerTutor.com Tactics Manager

Objective: Overcoming pressure on strong side and exploiting numerical advantage on weak side after switch.

Description

In this final practice of this session, we now play an 11 v 11 game with 5 zones marked out. The 2 end zones are 18 yards long and the 3 middle zones are split equally into vertical thirds.

After the goalkeeper receives, the white players adjust their shape (Bielsa's 3-3-3-1) and the centre back receives. The blue players shift towards the strong side to win possession and the whites try to find a way to either attack on the strong side (if the organisation of the blues is not good) or switch play towards the weak side (far 1/3 of the pitch) using the options that have been described in the previous practices within this session.

As soon as the ball is directed to the weak side's 1/3, the whites have 6-8 seconds to exploit the 3 v 2 or 2 v 1 advantage to dribble the ball through the red line or receive beyond it within the end zone and score versus the goalkeeper. If the blues win possession, they launch a counter attack and try to score within 8-10 seconds.

Restrictions: The blue winger and full back on the weak side (No.2 & 7 in diagram) should shift across to enter the central zone when pressing on the strong side. The blues are not allowed to defend within the end zone.

CHAPTER 3

BUILDING UP PLAY FROM THE BACK AGAINST 1 FORWARD

POSITIONING TO BUILD UP PLAY AGAINST 1 FORWARD

When the opposition are using a formation with 1 forward e.g. 4-2-3-1 or 4-3-3, there is a 2 v 1 situation at the back, as shown in the diagram below. So, unlike the previous chapter against 2 forwards, there is no need for a midfielder to drop back into the back line to create a numerical advantage. This means that Bielsa's initial formation (4-2-3-1) does not have to be changed as it was done when playing against 2 forwards.

Positioning and Formation Against 1 Forward (Bielsa's 4-2-3-1)

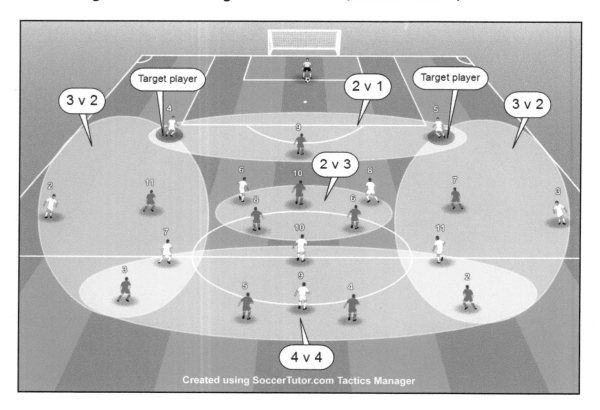

Created using SoccerTutor.com Tactics Manager

To demonstrate building up play against a team with 1 forward, the diagram show's Bielsa's 4-2-3-1 against an opposition (blues) also playing with a 4-2-3-1 formation.

There is a numerical advantage in the defensive line (2 v 1) which favours building up play from the goalkeeper without the need of any positional movements. In the centre of the pitch there is a 2 v 3 situation in favour of the defending team, while a 4 v 4 situation exists in the attacking line.

The interaction between the two formations (especially in the central area) depends on how deep or high the opposition's No.10 plays.

ASSESSMENT:

1. As a 3 v 2 numerical advantage exists near the sidelines, the 'target players' within Bielsa's 4-2-3-1 formation when building up play, are the 2 centre backs.

2. It is obvious that if the opposition No.10 (or most advanced midfielder) holds a deep and central position, it makes it more difficult to play passes from near the sidelines towards the inside or successfully switch the play through a central midfielder - this is much easier when playing against 2 forwards, as shown in the previous chapter.

STEP 1: PROVIDING A FREE PASSING OPTION FOR THE GOALKEEPER AGAINST 1 FORWARD

2 v 1 at the Back Against 1 Forward

The 2 v 1 numerical advantage at the back enables the goalkeeper to have an available passing option, as at least one of the centre backs will always be free.

There is no need for a midfielder to drop deep and no further action has to be taken from the attacking team.

STEP 2: MOVING THE BALL TO THE TARGET OR FREE PLAYER AGAINST 1 FORWARD

When the goalkeeper has the ball and the team are playing against 1 forward, the ball can be moved to the 'target player' with a direct pass. However, the 3 v 2 numerical advantage near the sideline can only be created if that target player (centre back) has overcome the potential pressure from the forward (9) or No.10 who is in a deeper position.

'Target Player' Receives and Overcomes Pressure to Create a 3 v 2 Numerical Advantage Near the Sideline

The centre back (4) receives a pass direct from the goalkeeper. As both the opposition forward (9) and the No.10 are too far away to put him under pressure, a 3 v 2 situation is created near the sideline.

However, if the 'target player' receives but No.9 and No.10 are able to shift quickly across to the strong side, then it becomes almost impossible to create a numerical advantage near the sideline - this is shown in the example on the next page.

The Opposition Forward Puts the 'Target Player' Under Pressure and Prevents the 3 v 2 Numerical Advantage Near the Sideline

Created using SoccerTutor.com Tactics Manager

In this example, as soon as the pass is made from the goalkeeper to the centre back (4), the forward (9) and the No.10 quickly shift across to that side. The blue forward (9) manages to catch the man in possession and put him under pressure.

In addition, the No.10 is able to shift across to the ball area and create a strong side for the defending team, with a 3 v 3 situation near the sideline and a 5 v 4 numerical advantage around the ball area.

This situation is a problem for Bielsa's teams when building up play from the back. Creating a numerical advantage on this side has now become impossible.

However, on the weak side (right side of diagram) there is a 3 v 2 numerical advantage in favour of the whites - the aim now becomes moving the ball to the other centre back and 'target player' No.5.

The different options Bielsa's teams use to switch the play to No.5 in this situation are shown in the next diagram example on page 61.

ASSESSMENT:

1. The movement of the central midfielder (8) who is away from the ball is very important in this situation, as he drops back to provide safety at the back in case possession is lost. Additionally, he can act as potential 'link player' for the centre back (4) or the midfielders No.7 and No.6 in a potential attempt to switch play - examples of this are shown on the next page.

2. It is the central midfielder closest to the weak side that drops back. It is the No.8 who drops back to provide cover in this example. If the No.6 dropped back in this situation, it would mean that No.4 would have one less passing option.

Options to Switch the Play in Limited Space and Create a Numerical Advantage on the Weak Side

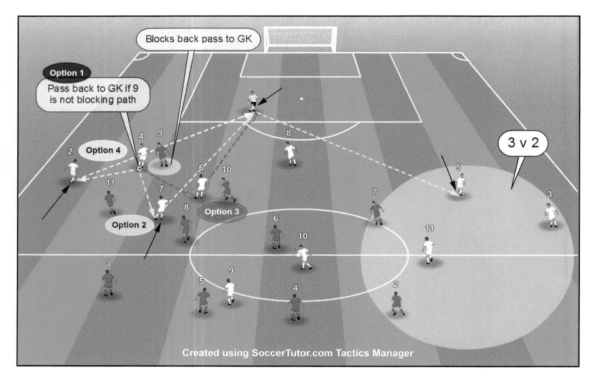

As already shown in the previous diagram, one of the strengths of formations with 1 forward when defending near the sideline is the fact that a strong side can be created by the quick shifting across of the forward (9) and the No.10 near to the ball area.

The blue forward (9) can potentially block the direct pass back to the goalkeeper and the pass inside to No.6. The No.10 can block potential passes from the centre back or full back towards the central midfielder (8) who has dropped back to receive and switch the play.

These are the 4 options that Bielsa's team use in this situation:

1. If the route is not blocked by blue No.9, the simplest option is the back pass to the goalkeeper *(this is not shown in the diagram above)*.

2. If the direct back pass to the goalkeeper is blocked by blue No.9, the potential pass towards the inside will probably be free. No.7 can become a 'link player' to move the ball to the goalkeeper or No.8. From there, the team can easily switch the play to No.5 and create a 3 v 2 numerical advantage near the sideline.

3. This is the same as option 2 but No.6 is used as the 'link player' instead of No.7.

4. If both the direct back pass to the goalkeeper and the inside pass are risky choices, the ball can be moved to the goalkeeper via the full back (2) who drops back, receives and passes back. The goalkeeper then passes to No.5, just like in the previous two options.

SESSION 4

Based on Tactics of Marcelo Bielsa

Playing Through Pressure on the Strong Side and Switching Play Against 1 Forward

SESSION FOR THIS TACTICAL SITUATION (2 PRACTICES)
1. Pattern of Play to Build Up and Switch the Play Against 1 Forward

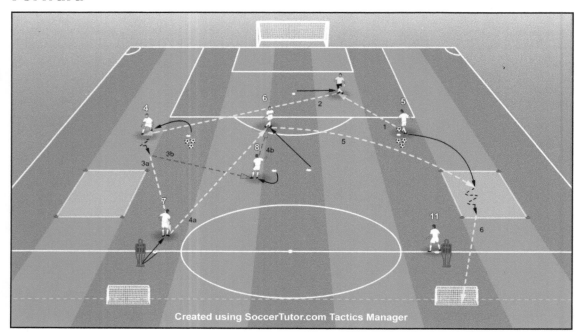

Created using SoccerTutor.com Tactics Manager

Objective: We work on the tactical aspects of playing through pressure on the strong side and switching play. The practice can be adapted to various formations.

Description

This practice is very similar to the one on page 45 - it is just adjusted to play against 1 forward and we add an extra central midfielder (6) who drops back to join the back three.

Using an area 10 yards longer than half a full pitch, we work with 6-12 outfield players. Using Bielsa's tactics, the players start with a 2-2-2 formation from the 4-2-3-1. We have 2 centre backs (4 & 5), 2 central midfielders (6 & 8 - one of which drops back) and 2 wingers (7 & 11) on the halfway line.

The practice starts with the left centre back (5) who passes to the goalkeeper. The goalkeeper then passes to the right centre back (4) who opens up, receives and plays the next pass. No.6 drops back to retain defensive balance.

At the same time, the winger (7) gets free of marking and the other central midfielder (8) provides a passing option, so No.4 has 2 options. Whichever player he passes to; they then pass back to No.6 as shown. As soon as No.6 receives, the centre back on the other side (5) moves forward, receives the long pass within the marked area and scores in the small goal. We then perform the same combination, starting with No.4's pass to the goalkeeper and his pass to No.5.

Coaching Points

1. Players need to focus on their timing - synchronising movements and approaching the ball on the move.
2. The central midfielder (8) must focus on producing accurate long passes which land inside the marked areas.

MARCELO BIELSA - BUILDING UP PLAY AGAINST HIGH PRESSING TEAMS

PROGRESSION

2. Playing Through Pressure on the Strong Side Against 1 Forward and Switching Play in an 8 (+GK) v 6 Game

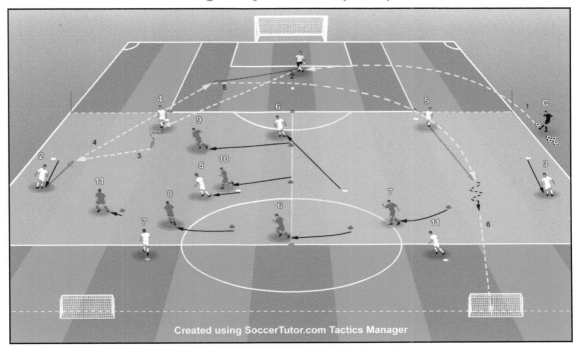

Created using SoccerTutor.com Tactics Manager

Description

This practice is very similar to the one on page 46 - it is just adjusted to play against 1 forward. Using 2/3 of a full pitch, we mark out the area between the halfway line and the penalty area. We have 1 full size goal with a goalkeeper and 2 small goals at the other end, as shown. The white team start with a 4-2-2 formation and adjust to 3-3-2 when No.6 drops back to cover - the blue team are in a 2-3-1 formation with 1 forward.

The practice starts with the coach's long pass to the goalkeeper. The white players move from the white cones and readjust their shape to counter the 2-3-1 formation. The goalkeeper passes to either No.4 or No.5 (No.6 drops back to retain balance). The blue forward (9) applies pressure to prevent a 3 v 2 situation on that side. The rest of the blue players shift towards the strong side and they have a numerical equality or advantage around the ball area. Their aim is to prevent the switch of play, win the ball and then score within 8-10 seconds.

The white team aim to find a solution to switch play towards the other side where they have a 2 v 1 situation. The 3 different options for No.4 are fully explained on page 61:

1. Direct pass back to goalkeeper who switches play to No.5.
2. Pass forward to No.7 who passes back to the goalkeeper.
3. Pass inside to No.8 who passes back to the goalkeeper.

Note - No.6 can also be used to switch play if the passing lane is available (as shown in the previous practice).

SESSION 5

Based on Tactics of
Marcelo Bielsa

Switching Play Against 1 Forward and Exploiting an Advantage on the Weak Side

SESSION FOR THIS TACTICAL SITUATION (4 PRACTICES)
1. Pattern of Play to Build Up and Switch the Play Against 1 Forward + Attacking Combinations

Created using SoccerTutor.com Tactics Manager

Description

This practice is a variation of the practice on Page 48, adjusted to the situation of playing against one forward - we add one more white central midfielder.

The practice starts with the coach's pass to the goalkeeper, who receives and moves towards one side, before passing to a centre back (No.4 in diagram), who opens up. To switch the play, the centre back has 4 options:

1. If the path is not blocked, the pass back to the goalkeeper is the easiest option - he acts as a 'link player' to switch play to No.5 in space *(see analysis on page 61)*.

2. If the direct path to the goalkeeper is blocked, the winger (No.7) drops back and acts as a 'link player' to switch play via the keeper or central midfielder No.6 *(see analysis on page 61 & diagram above)*.

3. This is the same as option 2 but the central midfielder (No.8) is used as the 'link player' to switch play via the keeper or the other central midfielder No.6 *(see analysis on page 61)*.

4. If the direct pass back to the goalkeeper and the inside pass are too risky, the full back drops back (No.2 in diagram) and acts as a 'link player' to switch play via the goalkeeper *(see analysis on page 61)*.

Which attacking combination the players then carry out depends on which area the pass is received in. The two different scenarios are as follows:

Scenario 1: Centre back (5) receives in the deepest area, moves forward and passes into the other area. The full back moves forward to receive the next pass and No.11 makes a run in behind the mannequin (defender) and into the end zone.

Scenario 2: This example is shown in the diagram and the central midfielder No.6 (or keeper) switches play. The full back (3) receives either from the centre back No.5 or directly from the switch of play and plays a 1-2 combination with No.11, and receives in behind the mannequin (defender).

Scenario 3: The last scenario is the full back (No.3 in diagram) receiving and No.11 making an overlapping run to receive in behind *(not shown in either diagram)*.

The team then try to score past the goalkeeper. The forward (9) times his run to try and finish.

Rules

1. The switch of play must be carried out at speed (within 6-8 seconds from the time the goalkeeper delivers the first pass).
2. The combination play on the weak side must also be finished within 6-8 seconds, from the time the long pass is received.

Coaching Points

1. Players need to focus on their timing - synchronised movements and approaching the ball on the move.
2. The central midfielder must focus on producing accurate long passes.
3. All actions have to be taken at speed.

PROGRESSION

2. Switching Play Against 1 Forward and Exploiting an Advantage on the Weak Side in a Functional Practice

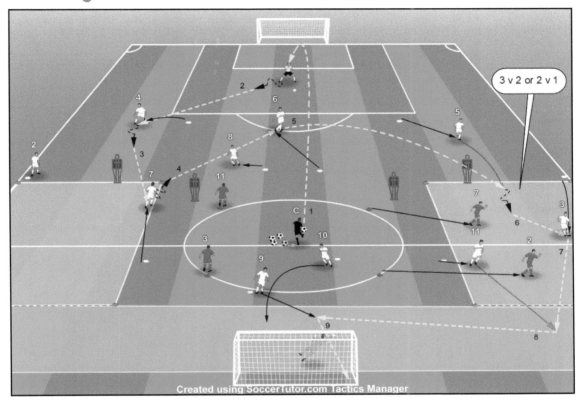

Description

Using 2/3 of a full pitch, we mark out 4 blue mannequins, 2 side zones and an end zone. The white team have 10 outfield players and the blues have 4 - there are 2 goalkeepers in full sized goals at either end.

The practice starts with the coach's pass to the goalkeeper, who receives and moves towards one side, before passing to a centre back (No.4 in diagram), who opens up. The ball should then be directed into the side zone and the whites use one of the combinations outlined in the previous practice *(also see analysis on page 61)* and switch the play to the weak side.

If the centre back receives (No.5 in diagram) after a switch of play, the whites have a 3 v 2 advantage in the side zone on the weak side. If the full back receives (No.3 in diagram), they have a 2 v 1 advantage. The aim is to dribble through the red line or receive a pass beyond it in the end zone.

For this they can use two different attacking combinations:

1. The full back (3) receives from the centre back (5) and the winger (11) makes a diagonal run in behind.
2. The full back (3) receives from the centre back (5) and plays a 1-2 combination with the winger (11), receiving in the end zone after making an overlapping run to exploit the 2 v 1 situation.

68

3. The full back (No.3 in diagram) receives in a 2 v 1 situation and draws in the defender (blue No.2) - white No.11 makes an overlapping run outside his teammate (full back) to receive a pass in behind (not shown in either diagram).

Restrictions

1. The white team have 6-8 seconds to exploit their numerical advantage in the side zone, from the time that the long pass (switch) is received.
2. The blues are not allowed to defend within the end zone.

Coaching Points

1. The white players have to read the tactical situation and carry out the appropriate combination to exploit the numerical advantage.
2. The exploitation of the numerical advantage should be done quickly and efficiently.

PROGRESSION

3. Switching Play Against 1 Forward and Exploiting an Advantage on the Weak Side in a Functional Game

4 v 5

Description

In this progression of the previous practice, we now have 10 white outfield players and 8 blue outfield players. There are 2 goalkeepers with full sized goals in 18 yard zones. All the players start on their respective cones and then adjust accordingly to the situation. The practice starts with the coach's pass to the goalkeeper, who passes to a centre back within a side zone (No.4 in diagram). There is a 4 v 5 situation (numerical disadvantage) with blue No.9 and No.10 shifting across. All the other blue players shift across to this side also and the blues aim to win the ball, and then score with a counter attack within 8-10 seconds.

The white team read the tactical situation and either attack on the strong side by dribbling the ball into the end zone or receiving a pass within it, before crossing and scoring - this is if the blues are not organised well. If this is not possible, the white team use the best option described in the previous 2 practices to switch play towards the weak side. The whites can then also use the attacking combinations used in the previous 2 practices after receiving the switch - trying to score with help from No.9 and No.10. Play on both sides.

Restrictions: The goalkeeper should direct the ball to the side the blue No.9 is on (blue No10 starts centrally). Blue players are not allowed to defend on the weak or inside the end zone area.

PROGRESSION

4. Switching Play Against 1 Forward and Exploiting an Advantage on the Weak Side in an 11 v 11 Zonal Game

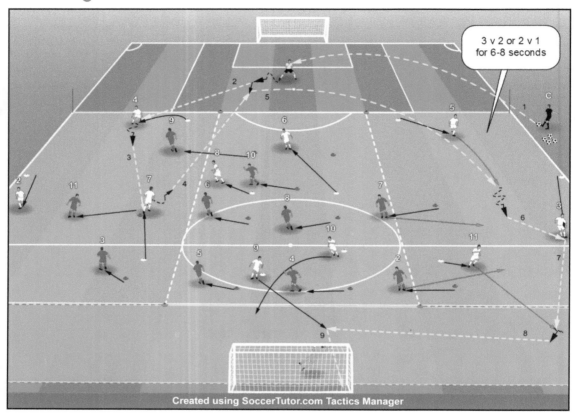

3 v 2 or 2 v 1 for 6-8 seconds

Created using SoccerTutor.com Tactics Manager

Description

In this final practice of this session, we now play an 11 v 11 game with 5 zones marked out. The 2 end zones are 18 yards long and the 3 middle zones are split equally into vertical thirds.

The goalkeeper receives, the white players adjust their shape and the centre back receives - the white central midfielder on the weak side (No.6 in diagram) drops deep to potentially help switch play and provide safety. The blue players shift towards the strong side to win possession and the whites try to switch play towards the weak side (far 1/3 of the pitch) using the options that have been described in the previous practices within this session.

As soon as the ball is directed to the weak side's 1/3, the whites have 6-8 seconds to exploit the 3 v 2 or 2 v 1 advantage to dribble the ball through the red line or receive beyond it within the end zone and score versus the goalkeeper. If the blues win possession, they launch a counter attack and try to score within 8-10 seconds.

Restrictions: The goalkeeper should direct the ball to the side the blue No.9 is on (blue No10 starts centrally). The blue winger and full back on the weak side (No.2 & 7 in diagram) should shift across to enter the central area when pressing on the strong side. The blues are not allowed to defend within the end zone.

CHAPTER 4

CREATING AND EXPLOITING 3 V 2 SITUATIONS NEAR THE SIDELINE

STEP 3: CREATING A NUMERICAL ADVANTAGE NEAR THE SIDELINE

This third step *'creating a numerical advantage near the sideline'* is related to *'providing a free passing option for the goalkeeper'* which was presented in step 1. As soon as the 'target player' manages to overcome the pressure of the closest 2 forwards or the forward and No.10, a 3 v 2 situation is created near the sideline.

Creating a 3 v 2 Numerical Advantage Near the Sidelines with the 4-2-3-1 Formation Against 2 Forwards

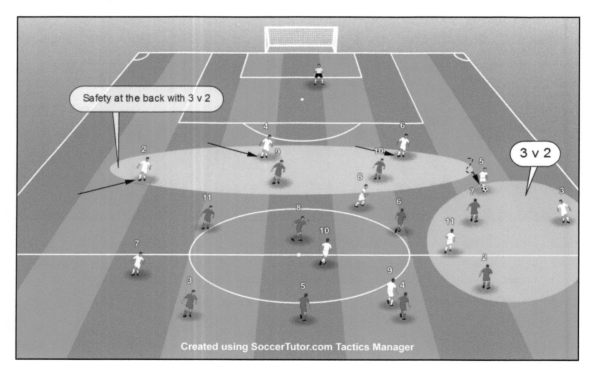

In this example, the centre back (5) has received the ball and moves forward (the central midfielder No.6 has moved into the back-line to provide cover).

The opposing forward on the strong side (blue No.10) is too away to apply pressure on the ball carrier, so the team have a 3 v 2 numerical advantage near the sideline, as shown in the diagram.

Simultaneously, the white players at the back (6, 4 & 2) shift towards the strong side - this creates a 3 v 2 numerical advantage at the back which ensures safety in case possession is lost.

Creating a 3 v 2 Numerical Advantage Near the Sidelines with the 4-2-3-1 Formation Against 1 Forward

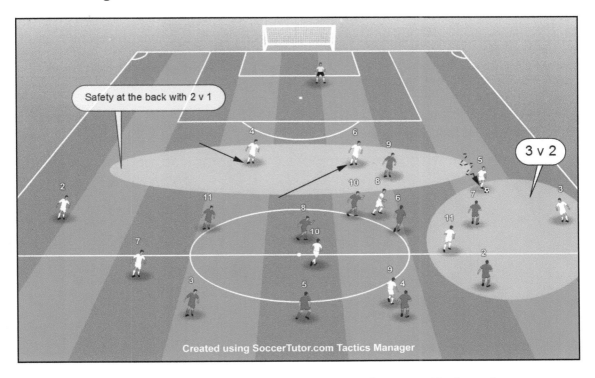

This is a variation of the previous example, with the opposition using a formation with 1 forward.

In this situation, if the blue forward (9) and No.10 are too far away from white No.5 to apply pressure, the same 3 v 2 numerical advantage can be created near the sideline, as shown in the diagram.

The central midfielder (6) again drops to cover No.5 as he moves forward, providing safety at the back.

STEP 4: EXPLOITING THE NUMERICAL ADVANTAGE CREATED

After creating a 3 v 2 situation near the sideline, Bielsa's tactics are to use this numerical advantage to move the ball to the free player. This can be done through intelligent positioning, good decision making and accurate passing. All the following options can be applied to all formations:

Option 1(a): Direct Pass to the Full Back Who is Free of Marking Near the Sideline

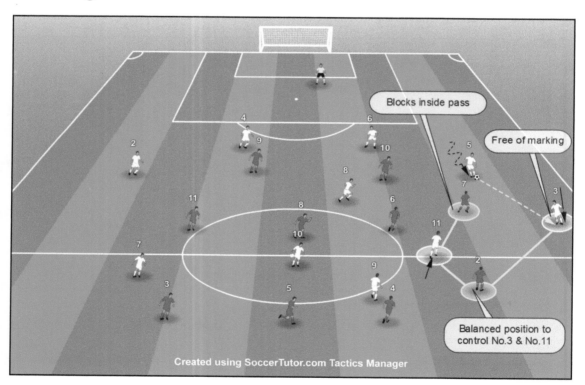

In this example, the winger (11) already has a central position and moves at the appropriate angle to provide a passing option. The left back (3) is in an effective position and at a good angle too. This positioning makes it impossible for the opposition winger (blue No.7) to block both passing options for the man in possession (5).

The centre back (5) has to decide which is the best passing option according to blue No.7's positioning. If blue No.7 decides to apply pressure in a way that blocks the inside pass towards white No.11, the pass towards the unmarked left back (3) is easy - this is shown in the diagram above.

Option 1(b): Exploiting the 2 v 1 with the Winger's Run into the Space Behind the Full Back

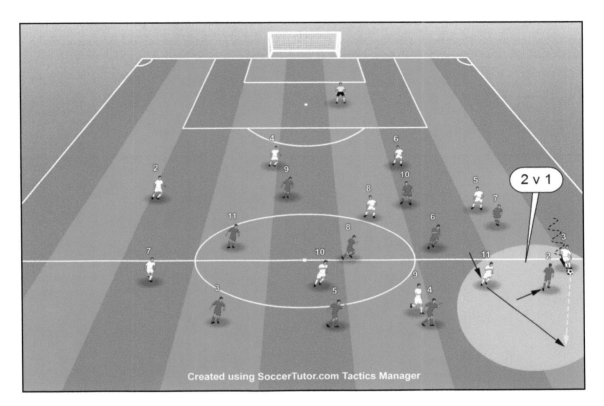

Created using SoccerTutor.com Tactics Manager

This diagram follows on from the example on the previous page. As soon as the left back (3) receives, he has available time on the ball and free space to move forward. This action creates a 2 v 1 numerical advantage near the sideline and a 5 v 4 advantage for the attack.

The aim for the team is to launch a quick attack from this point. This is to prevent the opposition midfielders from having enough time to get back and provide help to the defenders.

As we have a 2 v 1 situation in the highlighted area, the blue right back (2) has to move forward to contest the ball carrier. The winger (11) reads the situation and makes a diagonal run to receive in behind the blue right back, as shown in the diagram.

A successful pass to the winger (11) in this situation can lead to creating a goal scoring chance.

Option 1(c): The Winger Exploits the Space Created in the Centre by the Forward's Run Out Wide

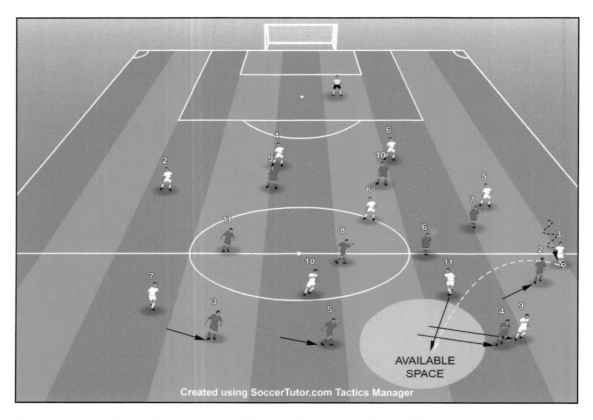

This is a variation of the previous example and shows a different option for the full back and winger when they have a numerical advantage near the sideline.

In this example, the forward (9) helps to create space. The forward (9) shifts towards the sideline to provide a passing option and his marker (blue centre back No.4) follows him. This reaction by the blue centre back creates free space in the centre of the blue team's defence.

The left winger (11) reads the tactical situation and makes a forward run into the available space created by the forward's run out wide. The left back (3) passes into the space for No.11 to run onto.

As in the previous example, a successful pass to the winger (11) in this situation can again lead to creating a goal scoring chance.

Option 2: Quick Combination Play to Move the Ball to the Free Full Back When the Direct Pass is Blocked

Blocks direct pass to No.3

Link player

Waits for the pass to be made & then puts pressure to avoid creating space behind

Created using SoccerTutor.com Tactics Manager

For the second option, the opposition winger (7) applies pressure in a different way and this time blocks the direct pass to our left back (3). As explained before, blue No.7 is unable to block both passing options, so this leaves our left winger (11) free of marking, ready to receive a pass from the centre back in possession (5).

In this situation, the reaction of the opposition right back (2) is the key. There are 3 possibilities:

- **Option 2** *(diagram above)*: If the blue right back (2) waits for the pass to be made and then moves to put pressure on the ball by taking advantage of the transmission phase (the time the ball takes to travel), the white winger (11) may not be able to receive and turn. However, the winger (11) can play as 'link player' in order to move the ball to the left back (3) who is free of marking.

  After the pass towards No.3 is achieved, both the options shown on the previous two pages can be used (option 1b: 'exploiting the 2 v 1 with the winger's run into the space behind the full back' and option 1c: 'the winger exploits the space created in the centre by forward's run out wide').

- **Option 3** *(page 79)*: The blue right back (2) retains a balanced position and does not move forward to contest our winger (11) which allows him to receive and turn - this is option 3 described on the next page.

- **Option 4** *(page 80)*: The blue right back (2) moves forward to contest the winger before the pass is made so he is unable to receive. The left back (3) must move forward into the free space.

Option 3: The Winger is Able to Receive in Space and Turn with 2 Passing Options

In this third option, the opposition winger (7) applies pressure in a way and that blocks the direct pass to our left back (3), as shown in option 2 on the previous page. As blue No.7 is unable to block both passing options, this leaves our left winger (11) free of marking, ready to receive a pass from the centre back in possession (5).

In option 2, the opposition right back (2) moved forward to prevent our winger (11) from turning. In this example, he doesn't move forward to put pressure on white No.11 after the centre back's (5) pass, but instead stays in a balanced position to control both No.11 and the left back No.3.

This enables the winger (11) to receive the pass from the centre back unmarked, turn and move forward with the ball. As soon as he is able to do this, the opposition midfielders are taken out of the game and we can launch a quick 5 v 4 attack.

A 2 v 1 situation is created again near the sideline. The winger (11) has 2 options:

1. Pass to the left back (3) who makes an overlapping run.

2. The winger can use the distraction of the left back's run to give him enough time and space to play a through pass in behind the defensive line in the centre. Another attacking player (No.10 in diagram) must make a well-timed run to meet this pass.

Option 4: Exploiting the Space Behind the Opposition Full Back Who Moves Forward to Mark Our Winger

In this final example, the blue right back (2) moves forward to mark our winger (11) before the pass is made so he is unable to receive. This prevents the centre back (5) from being able to pass to him. However, this early forward movement of the blue right back (2) creates space behind him.

If the man in possession (5) has enough time on the ball to play an aerial pass, the available space can be exploited by the forward run of the left back (3), as shown in the diagram.

In this situation, the white team would have a 4 v 3 numerical advantage for their attack and a good chance to create a goal scoring opportunity.

SESSION 6

Based on Tactics of Marcelo Bielsa

Creating and Exploiting 3 v 2 Situations Near the Sideline

SESSION FOR THIS TACTICAL SITUATION (8 PRACTICES)
1. Moving into Available Passing Lanes with Quick Combination Play (Unopposed)

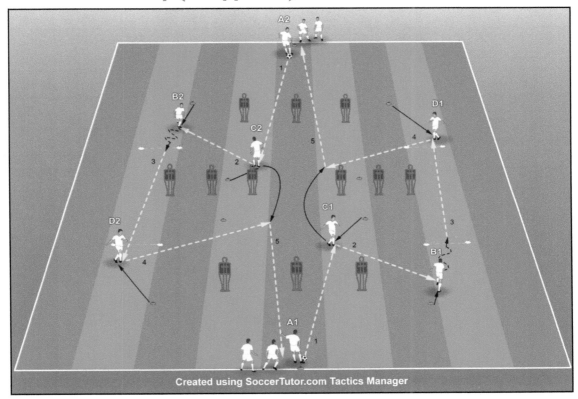

Created using SoccerTutor.com Tactics Manager

Objective: Pass/receive at different angles - focus on timing movement into available passing lanes.

Description

In a 35 x 50 yard area, we have 12 players, 2 balls (1 at either end as shown), 12 blue mannequins (or large cones), 4 white cone gates and 10 red cones to mark out starting positions.

The practice starts simultaneously with players A1 and A2 at opposite ends. We will explain the sequence starting from A1 - this is replicated on the other side, as shown. Player A1 passes to C1 who drops back and passes into the path of B1 who dribbles forward through the white cone gate. Player B1 then passes forward to D1 who has dropped back towards the available passing lane to provide a passing option. While this has been happening, player C1 has made a curved run to receive the next pass from D1. When he does, he passes to the second start position (A2) and the sequence continues with the next player.

All players move to the next position (A -> B -> C -> D -> Start).

Coaching Points

1. Move towards the passing lanes to receive the forward passes at the right moment.
2. Time the movement around the mannequins to receive the lay-off on the move.

82

VARIATION

2. Synchronised Movements and Combination Play Between the Full Back and Winger (Unopposed)

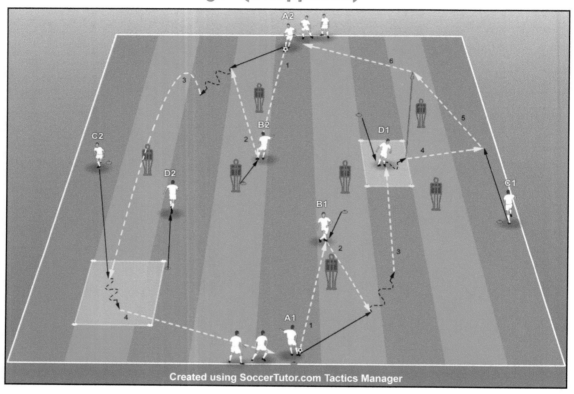

Created using SoccerTutor.com Tactics Manager

Description

This is a variation of the previous practice - the positions of the red cones and the blue mannequins (or large cones) change, as shown in the diagram. We also mark out 2 areas - one is 4 x 6 yards and the other is 5 x 8 yards.

The practice starts simultaneously with players A1 and A2 at opposite ends. On the right side, A1 plays a one-two combination with B1 who drops back - A1 receives back, dribbles forward and passes into the small area where D1 (winger) drops back to receive and turn. At the same time, C1 (full back) makes a run forward to receive out wide. To complete the sequence on this side, C1 passes at an angle for D1 who makes a run inside the mannequin and passes to the second start position (A2).

On the left side, A2 plays a one-two combination with B2 who drops back (D2 drops back and C2 moves forward) - A2 receives back, dribbles forward and plays an aerial pass into the larger area, into the path of C2. C2 finishes the sequence by passing to the A1 start position and the practice continues. All players move to the next position (A -> B -> C - > D -> Start).

Variations

1. The practice can be reversed so the players work on these combinations for the left side of the pitch.
2. Player D1 can use 1 touch to pass to C and move behind the mannequin to receive again (instead of turning).

83

PROGRESSION

3. Synchronised Movements and Combination Play Between the Full Back and Winger (Opposed)

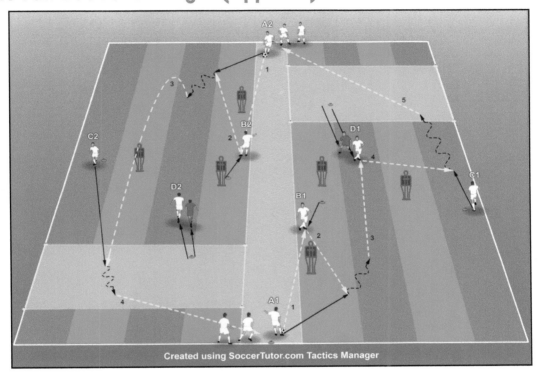

Created using SoccerTutor.com Tactics Manager

Description

This is a progression of the previous practice in the same 35 x 50 yard area - the same combinations between the full back and winger are used but now we have an opposing full back. We also have a 4-5 yard central channel and 2 marked out areas (10 x 15 yards,) each with a white winger (D) and a blue full back inside.

The practice starts simultaneously with players A1 and A2 at opposite ends who both play a one-two combination with B1 and B2 respectively, receive back, dribble forward and then look to play a pass - D1 and D2 drop back to provide a passing option. The players in possession have to read the tactical situation (which is determined by the blue player's reaction) in order to make the best choice:

1. The blue full back doesn't follow the winger (D1/D2) when they drop back, so D1/D2 can receive, turn and create a 2 v 1 situation inside the marked area *(not shown in diagram)*.
2. The blue full back follows the winger (D1/D2), so space is created for the white full back (C1/C2) to receive an aerial pass into the marked area *(shown on left side of diagram)*.
3. The blue full back waits for the pass to be made and then moves to put pressure on the winger (D1/D2), so the winger passes first time into the path of the full back (C1/C2) and there is a 2 v 1 situation inside the marked area *(shown on right side of diagram)*.

Each combination ends with a pass to the A1/A2 position and the sequence continues. All players move to the next position. The practice can be reversed so players work on these combinations for the left side of the pitch.

84

PROGRESSION

4. Playing to the Free Player in a 3 v 1 Tactical Situation Near the Sideline

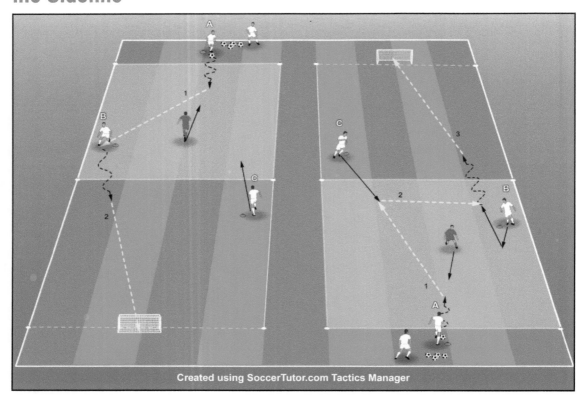

Created using SoccerTutor.com Tactics Manager

Objective: We work on taking advantage of a 3 v 1 tactical situation near the sideline.

Description

We mark out 2 separate playing areas (20 x 60 yards each) split into 2 halves. The 2 groups work in opposite directions simultaneously and each group has 5 players - white centre back (A), full back (B) and winger (C) + 1 blue defender. There is also an extra white player outside, waiting to take part.

A, B and C start on the red cones. Player A starts the practice by dribbling the ball forward and the blue defender moves to apply pressure. The aim for the white team is to pass the ball to the free player B, either directly or via the link player (C) - the decision making depends on the positioning of the blue defender:

1. Left side of diagram - if the blue defender is unable to block the pass towards the full back (B), then A can pass directly to him. B then dribbles forward and tries to score.

2. Right side of diagram - if player A is unable to find an angle to pass directly to B, he has the option of passing to C (link player) who drops back to create a passing option and move the ball to B.

All players move to the next position (A -> B -> C -> Start). The practice can be reversed so players work on these combinations for the left side of the pitch. Only player B can enter the attacking half with the ball.

PROGRESSION

5. Playing to the Free Player in a 3 v 2 Tactical Situation Near the Sideline

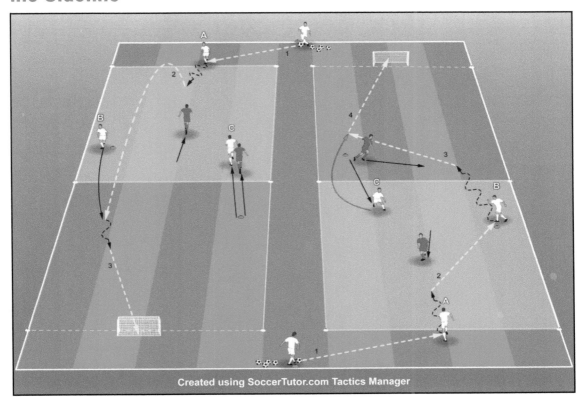

Created using SoccerTutor.com Tactics Manager

Description

This is a progression of the previous practice - we now add an extra defender so we have a 3 v 2 situation in each group. To start the practice, the outside player now passes to player A who enters the area.

Depending on the reactions of the 2 blue defenders, the aim for the white team is to use their numerical advantage to dribble the ball into the attacking half or receive a pass within it, then score. Two examples of combinations are shown in the diagram:

1. Left side of diagram - the first blue defender closes down the ball carrier (A) and the second defender follows the winger's (C) movement to drop back. This creates space for the full back to move forward, receive in the attacking half and score a goal.

2. Right side of diagram - the first blue defender does not block the direct pass to the full back (B) so a 2 v 1 situation is created straight away. The second defender moves to close down B who dribbles forward and plays a pass into the path of C, who makes a curved run in behind - he then scores a goal.

All white players move to the next position (A -> B -> C -> Start). The practice can be reversed so players work on these combinations for the left side of the pitch. Only player B can enter the attacking half with the ball.

PROGRESSION

6. Creating and Exploiting a 3 v 2 Numerical Advantage Near the Sideline in a Functional Practice

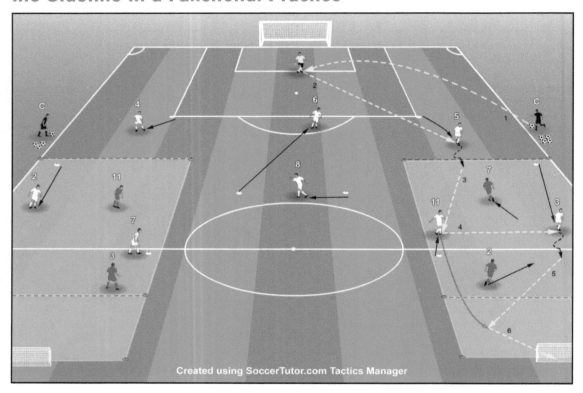

Created using SoccerTutor.com Tactics Manager

Objective: We work on taking advantage of a 3 v 2 tactical situation near the sideline.

Description

Using 2/3 of a full pitch we mark out 2 zones near the sidelines as shown. Within each zone we have a full back and a winger for both teams - there is an end zone within the zone and a goal. Outside of the zones, we have 2 white centre backs (4 & 5) and 2 central midfielders (6 & 8). The white players start on the white cones.

The practice starts when the coach plays a long ball towards the goalkeeper and the players adjust their shape to a 3-3-2 (from Bielsa's 3-3-3-1) as if building up play against 2 forwards. The 2 centre backs (4 & 5) move out wide to receive and the central midfielder (6) moves back to create a back three.

After a centre back receives (No.5 in diagram), he moves into the side zone on that side and the aim for the whites is to take advantage of the 3 v 2 situation, to either dribble the ball through the red end line or receive a pass beyond it and score within 8 seconds. The blues cannot defend behind the red line and the offside rule is applied throughout.

If the blue players win possession, they launch a counter attack and must dribble the ball through the opposite red end line or receive a pass beyond it within 5 seconds (1 goal). The midfielder in the centre (8) can enter the side zones when the white team are in a negative transition.

PROGRESSION

7. Creating and Exploiting a 3 v 2 Numerical Advantage Near the Sideline in an 11 v 10 Game

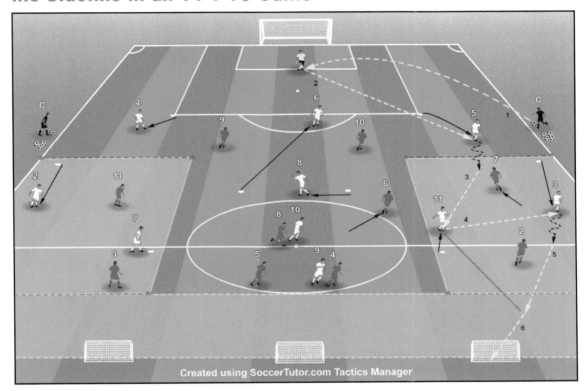

Created using SoccerTutor.com Tactics Manager

Description

Using the same set up as the previous practice, the end zone now goes across the full width of the pitch (15 yards long) and there are 3 goals at the end.

The practice starts when the coach plays a long ball towards the goalkeeper and the players adjust their shape to a 3-3-2 (from Bielsa's 3-3-3-1) to build up play against 2 forwards. The 2 centre backs (4 & 5) move out wide to receive and the central midfielder (6) moves back to create a back three.

The two teams play a normal game but when a white centre back (No.5 in diagram) enters a side zone, the aim is to take advantage of the 3 v 2 situation, to either dribble the ball through the red end line or receive a pass beyond it and score within 5-6 seconds. A goal scored this way counts double.

The 2 blue forwards don't actively try to prevent the white centre backs from entering the side zones. After that, the blue players defend, try to win the ball and then score within 8-10 seconds. The blues cannot defend in the end zone and the offside rule is applied throughout.

Coaching Point: The focus for the white team is to choose the appropriate solution, according to the reaction of the blue players *(see page 86 for attacking options)*.

MARCELO BIELSA - BUILDING UP PLAY AGAINST HIGH PRESSING TEAMS

PROGRESSION

8. Creating and Exploiting a 3 v 2 Numerical Advantage Near the Sideline in an 11 v 11 Game

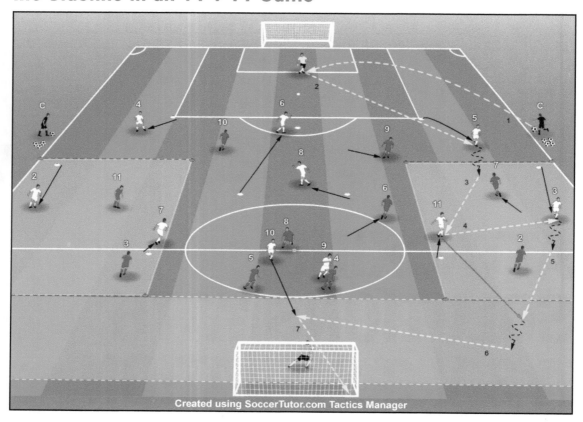

Created using SoccerTutor.com Tactics Manager

Description

This is a progression of the previous practice and the same rules/restrictions are applied.

We increase the length of the end zone to 25 yards and add a full sized goal with a goalkeeper. The white team still try to exploit a 3 v 2 advantage out wide, but now look to cross and finish in the large goal. The blues still defend, try to win the ball and counter attack to score against the other goalkeeper.

ASSESSMENT:

The practices in this session can all be adjusted to various formations.

CHAPTER 5

ATTACKING SOLUTIONS WITH A 3 V 3 SITUATION NEAR THE SIDELINE

ATTACKING SOLUTIONS WITH A 3 v 3 SITUATION NEAR THE SIDELINE (AGAINST 2 FORWARDS)

When our centre back moves forward with the ball and an opposition forward is unable to put pressure on him, we should be able to outnumber the opposition 3 v 2 situation near the sideline. However, opposition teams can prevent this by shifting one of their central midfielders across - this player then takes responsibility to close down the centre back in possession, while the opposition winger can track the forward run of our full back.

Opposition Prevent the 3 v 2 with the Extensive Shift of the Central Midfielder

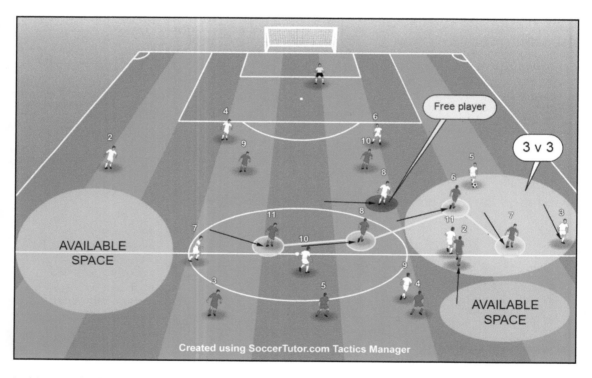

In this example, the opposition forwards are too far away from the ball carrier (centre back No.5) to apply pressure. The only way for the blue team to prevent a numerical disadvantage occurring near the sideline is for their central midfielder (6) to shift quickly across, as shown in the diagram - he then moves to close down No.5.

This reaction by blue No.6 triggers the extensive shifting of all the blue midfielders towards the strong side in order for midfield cohesion to be obtained and through passes to be blocked.

This reaction however, creates available space on the weak side for the white team, as well as space behind the blue right back (2), as he moves to close down his direct opponent white No.11.

Additionally, the white central midfielder (8) stays free of marking and he is the key player in this situation, as he can receive in space and pick the right pass.

3 v 3 Near the Sideline: Moving the Ball to the Free Central Midfielder

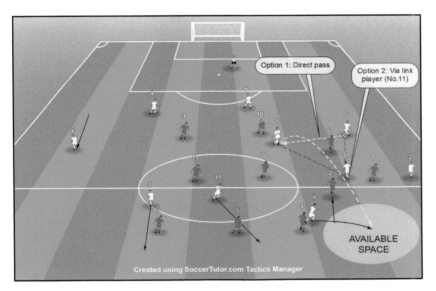

Option 1: Direct pass

Option 2: Via link player (No.11)

AVAILABLE SPACE

Following on from the previous page, the opposition have been able to create a 3 v 3 situation near the sideline.

As blue No.6 moves to close down the ball carrier, white No.8 is the free player. He can either receive a direct pass from No.5 or via the 'link player' No.11, as shown. No.8 can then play a long pass into the space behind blue No.2, which can be a very effective option if the forward (9) is a fast player. If he can get to the ball first, there will be a 3 v 3 situation for the attack.

Switching Play to Exploit the Space on the Weak Side

Midfield cohesion blocks through passes

2 v 1

This diagram shows an alternative option for No.8 when he receives from No.5. The opposition's midfield is compact. There is more space and less accuracy needed.

As shown, No.8 can switch play towards the weak side, where the left back (3) has plenty of space to receive.

After the left back (3) receives the ball, there is a good opportunity to create a 2 v 1 situation near the sideline, with No.7 making a diagonal run into the space behind the blue left back (3).

Playing the Through Pass when the Opposition Midfield is not Compact

Stays wider to deny space on weak side and leaves gap in centre

3 v 3 situation with an overload within blue No.3's zone of responsibility (red area)

Created using SoccerTutor.com Tactics Manager

In this variation of the previous example, the blue left winger (11) is in a wider position to prevent white No.8 from switching the play and creating a 2 v 1 situation on the weak side.

However, this wider position means that there is less midfield cohesion and compactness for the blue team. As a result of this, a through pass can be played by No.8.

Additionally, the positioning of white No.10 is within the opposition left back's (3) zone of responsibility (red area in diagram). As white No.7 is also in his zone of responsibility (2 v 1), he cannot move forward to mark No.10 and must leave him to receive the pass from white No.8 in space.

White No.10 can receive, turn and make a final pass in behind the opposition's defensive line, with his team in a favourable 3 v 3 situation for the attack.

ATTACKING SOLUTIONS WITH A 3 v 3 SITUATION NEAR THE SIDELINE (AGAINST 1 FORWARD)

When playing against teams with 1 forward, it is likely that there will be a No.10 or attacking midfielder who would be deeper than a second forward and would prevent the central midfielder (8) receiving in a central area.

When playing against 1 forward, a central midfielder does not need to drop back between the 2 centre backs to create a back three but one central midfielder does still drop into a deep position to receive a pass from the centre back. He can then switch play as shown in the previous pages against 2 forwards.

As well as providing a useful passing option back, the central midfielder also provides safety at the back and retains a numerical advantage (2 v 1 or 3 v 1) against the opposition forward.

Opposition's Compact Midfield Creates Space Near the Sideline to Switch Play

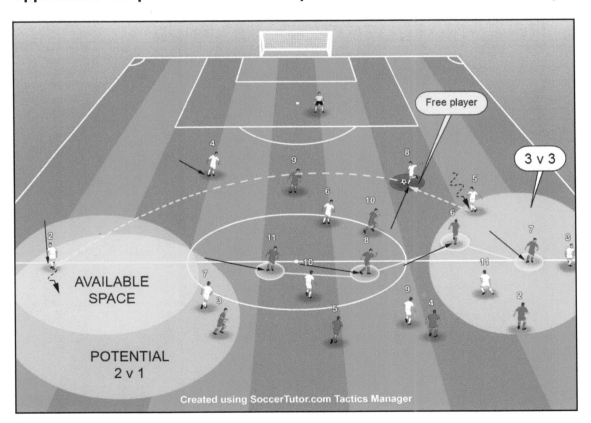

In this example, the blue defending team prevent a 3 v 2 disadvantage being created near the sideline with the extensive shift of the central midfielder (6) who moves to close down the ball carrier and they have a compact midfield. The available space on the other side can be exploited by No.5's back pass to the central midfielder (8) who switches play towards the full back (2) in the available space. This can create a potential 2 v 1 situation.

Playing the Through Pass When the Opposition Midfield is Not Compact

3 v 3

Stays wide to deny space

No midfield cohesion allows
through pass to No.10

Created using SoccerTutor.com Tactics Manager

If the blue winger (No.11 in diagram) is in a wider position to prevent the white team switching play into space, the blue team's midfield cohesion will suffer.

In this example, there is a large gap between blue No.11 and No.8. The white central midfielder (8) passes inside to No.6 this time and he is able to play a forward pass through the gap in midfield, to No.10. The blue midfielders are now taken out of the game and there is at least a 4 v 4 situation for an attack.

No.10 can receive, turn and play a final ball to create a goal scoring opportunity.

ASSESSMENT:

These situations can take place if the blue forward is positioned away from the ball area. If he is close and a strong side is created for the blue team, then a switch of play should be obtained with the potential options that have already been mentioned.

SESSION 7

Based on Tactics of Marcelo Bielsa

Attacking Solutions to Counter the 3 v 3 Situation Near the Sideline

SESSION FOR THIS TACTICAL SITUATION (4 PRACTICES)
1. Quick Combination to Switch Play to the Full Backs in Available Space (Technical Practice)

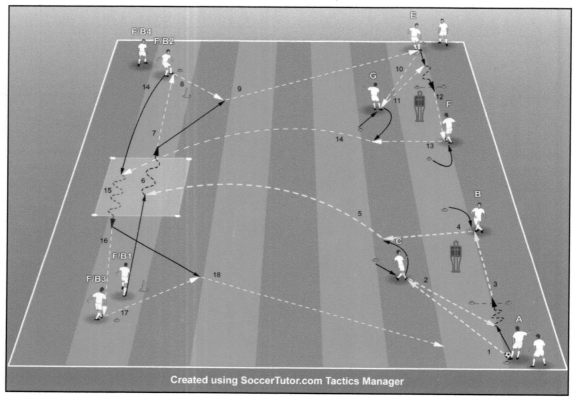

Created using SoccerTutor.com Tactics Manager

Description

In a 60 x 60 yard area, we have 12 players, 2 mannequins (or large cones), 4 cone gates and extra cones to mark out starting positions. We have 3 groups of players - the first 2 groups represent the centre back (A) and midfielders (B & C). The third group is made of full backs (2 at each end) separated by an 8 x 8 yard area.

The practice starts with player A's pass to C, who lays the ball back to A. Player A then dribbles the ball through the cone gate and passes forward to B who drops back. Player B passes inside to C who moves to receive and play a long pass to the other side (switching play) into the 8 x 8 yard area for a full back.

The full back (F/B1) has moved forward and receives within the area, dribbles forward, plays a 1-2 combination with the second full back (F/B2) and then passes to player E.

The same combination is then carried out with E, F and G as it was with A, B and C, before the ball is switched into the 8 x 8 yard area again, this time to F/B2. F/B2 then plays a 1-2 combination with F/B3 and passes back to the start position (A) and the practice continues. Full backs swap sides every time they receive a pass and the other players rotate positions (A -> B -> C -> Start).

Coaching Point: C & G need to move at the right moment to receive the lay-off pass and switch play first time.

PROGRESSION

2. Attacking Solutions to Counter the 3 v 3 Situation Near the Sideline in a Zonal Game (Against 2 Forwards)

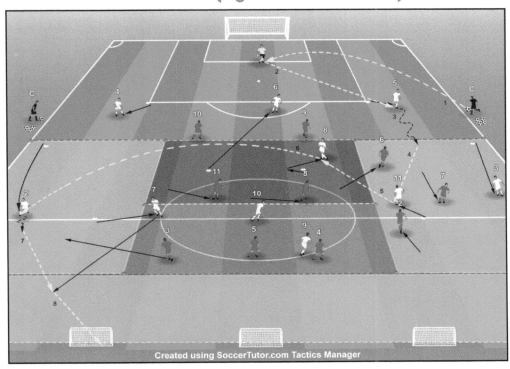

Created using SoccerTutor.com Tactics Manager

Description

Using 2/3 of a full pitch, we divide the area into 6 zones as shown in the diagram. There is 1 full size goal with a goalkeeper at one end and 3 small goals at the other end.

The practice always starts when the coach plays a long ball towards the goalkeeper and the players adjust their shape (Bielsa's 3-3-3-1) to build up play against 2 forwards. The 2 centre backs (4 & 5) move out wide to receive, the central midfielder (6) moves back to create a back three and the full backs (2 & 3) push up.

When the goalkeeper passes to one of the centre backs (No.5 in diagram), the blues can either allow a 3 v 2 or create a 3 v 3 inside the side zone (if they want) with the extensive shift of the central midfielder (blue No.6).

The white team have to read the situation (according to the reaction of the blues) and either exploit the 3 v 2 or counter the 3 v 3 by taking advantage of the available space on the weak side, or by playing a through pass to No.7, No.10 or No.11 within their blue zone - they can then exploit a 3 v 3 attack. To score, they must dribble through the red end line or receive beyond it, and then pass/shoot into any of the 3 small goals.

If the blues win the ball in a side zone, they must dribble the ball through the red line (1 goal). If they win the ball in the centre, they try to score past the goalkeeper within 8-10 seconds.

Restrictions: The blue players are not allowed to defend in the end zone and the blue forwards (9 & 10) must stay within their zone when their team is defending.

VARIATION

3. Attacking Solutions to Counter the 3 v 3 Situation Near the Sideline in a Zonal Game (Against 1 Forward)

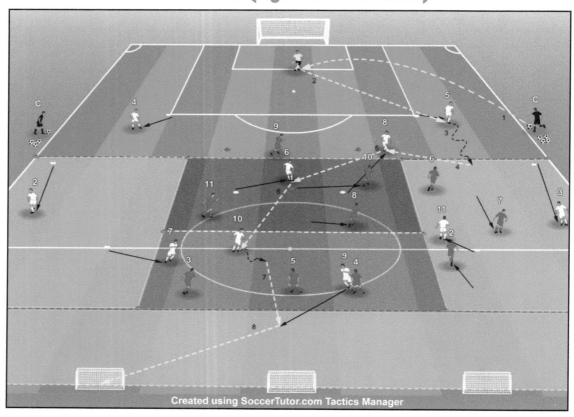

Description

In this variation of the previous practice, we adjust to play against a team with 1 forward. The same aims and rules apply. The first central midfielder (6) doesn't drop back as the opposition only have 1 forward (2 v 1).

In this practice against 1 forward, there will always be a 3 v 3 situation in the side zone that the centre back enters (No.5 in diagram). The solutions are fully explained on pages 94-95:

* Page 94: The opposition's compact midfield creates space near the sideline to switch play (blue No.11 is positioned inside). When No.8 receives from No.5, he plays a long pass to switch the play towards the full back (2) who has plenty of space.

* Page 95 *(as shown in diagram):* Play a through pass when the opposition midfield is not compact (blue No.11 stays wide to prevent switch of play). A forward (No.10 in diagram) is able to receive, turn and attack.

Coaching Points

1. The midfielder must make the right decision (switch play or through pass) to create a favourable situation.
2. After receiving switch of play or through pass, play quickly to exploit numerical advantage (in centre or wide).

99

4. Attacking Solutions to Counter the 3 v 3 Situation Near the Sideline in an 11 v 11 Zonal Game

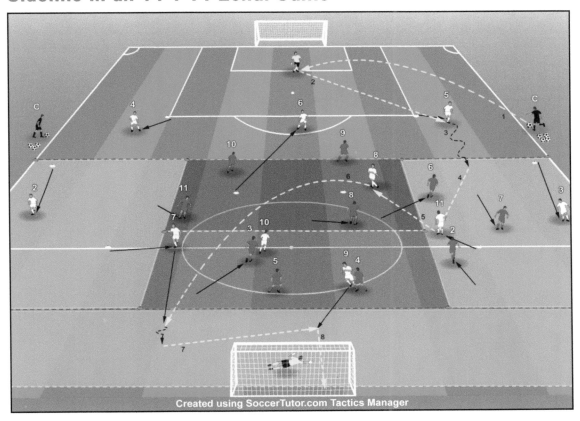

Created using SoccerTutor.com Tactics Manager

Description

This is a progression of the previous 2 practices and the same objectives, rules and restrictions apply. We now play an 11 v 11 game with 2 full sized goals and goalkeepers. The white team try to use their numerical advantage at the back to receive and then create a 3 v 2 numerical advantage in one of the side zones. If the blues prevent this and create a 3 v 3 situation, then the whites use the same solutions as explained in the tactical analysis section of this chapter and the 2 previous practices.

In the diagram example, a 3 v 3 situation occurs in the side zone and the No.8 is the free player again. The ball is moved to No.8 via No.11 (the link player). Once No.8 receives, No.10 moves towards the passing lane to provide a passing option and is followed by his marker (blue left back No.3). This creates available space behind blue No.3 which the white No.7 notices and makes a forward run. No.8 plays a long pass into the available space and No.7 receives in behind and passes across goal to No.9 for the whites to score. The blue team defend, try to win possession and then score within 8 – 10 seconds.

Restrictions: Blue players are not allowed to defend in the end zone and the blue forwards (9 & 10) must stay within their zone when their team is defending.

CHAPTER 6

CREATING AND EXPLOITING SPACE IN A 4 V 3 (OR 4 V 4) SITUATION AROUND THE BALL AREA

CREATING AND EXPLOITING SPACE IN A 4 v 3 (or 4 v 4) SITUATION AROUND THE BALL AREA

If the ball is moved to the 'free player' instead of the 'target player' (Bielsa's defensive minded 3-4-3 option for building up play against 2 forwards), tactical adjustments should be made in order for the attacking team to create superiority in numbers around the ball area. This is related to pages 24-25 if you wish to refer back as a reference.

Changing a 3 v 3 Situation to 4 v 3 Near the Sideline with the Forward Shifting Across (Bielsa's 3-4-3 Defensive Option)

No.9's shift changes the situation from 3 v 3 to 4 v 3

Created using SoccerTutor.com Tactics Manager

this situation, the right centre back (4) receives a pass from the goalkeeper and there is originally a 3 v 3 tion on that side. To change the situation from 3 v 3 to 3 v 4 and create a numerical advantage around the rea, the forward (9) drops back and across (as shown in the diagram).

his shift from the forward (9), if the opposition winger (blue No.11) decides to close down the man in ssion (white No.4), the white team can use almost all of the potential combinations that were described in *r 3: Creating and Exploiting 3 v 2 Situations Near the Sideline'* to create and exploit a 3 v 2 near the sideline, orward (9) takes over the role of a midfielder.

ASSESSMENT:

If the opposition (blues) want to prevent a 3 v 2 situation being created behind their winger (11), their central midfielder (8) may take over the responsibility of closing down the man in possession (white No.4).

The solution for the white team in this situation would be different - they would then have space to switch the play or make a through pass (depending on the level of midfield cohesion and compactness of the blues), as it was described in the previous chapter.

Opposition Centre Back Follows the Forward's Movement Which Creates a 4 v 4 Situation, So the No.10 Makes a Run in Behind Him

If the opposition try to prevent the numerical advantage created in the example on the previous page, it would most likely be the centre back (5) who follows our forward's (9) movement to mark him closely - this then creates a 4 v 4 situation as shown, meaning an equality in numbers around the ball area.

However, this movement by blue No.5 creates a big gap in the centre of the opposition's defence. This space can then be exploited if No.10 makes a movement into the available space to receive an accurate long pass by the man in possession (No.4).

This option can be very effective if No.10 is a fast player. He could potentially be in on goal or at least create a 2 v 2 situation for the attack - white No.10 and No.11 versus blue No.4 and No.2.

SESSION 8

Based on Tactics of Marcelo Bielsa

Creating and Exploiting Space in a 4 v 3 (or 4 v 4) Situation Around the Ball Area

SESSION FOR THIS TACTICAL SITUATION (4 PRACTICES)
1. Creating and Exploiting Space in Behind in a Technical Practice

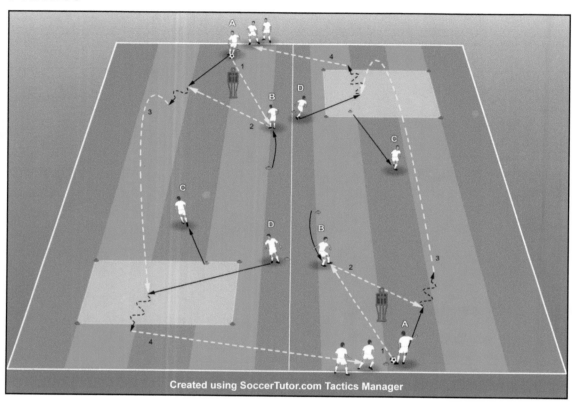

Created using SoccerTutor.com Tactics Manager

Objective

Technical training to practice playing a long pass and timing a run to receive it within a restricted area.

Description

In a 40 x 60 yard area we have 12 players, 2 mannequins (or large cones) and 8 red cones which mark the starting positions. The pitch is split down the middle and we have 2 small 10 x 8 yard areas at opposite ends, as shown.

The practice starts simultaneously with 2 balls - one each with both player As. Player A plays a 1-2 combination round the mannequin (defender) with B who drops back. Before A receives the ball back, player C drops back to create space behind him and D starts his movement towards the 10 x 8 yard area. Player A then plays a long pass for D who must receive within the area and then pass to player A on the opposite side.

The practice runs simultaneously on the other side with the exact same combination, so the ball is transferred from one group to the other. All players move to the next position (A -> B -> C -> D -> Opposite Side).

The practice can be reversed to train the players on the left side too. The size of the receiving area can be changed, depending on the age/level of the players.

PROGRESSION

2. Creating and Exploiting Space Within a 4 v 3 or 4 v 4 Situation in a Dynamic Zonal Practice

Description

In a 55 x 60 yard area, we divide the pitch into 6 zones. The 4 larger zones are all 25 x 30 yards and the 2 middle zones are 5 x 30 yards. There are also small red zones on either side, which are just used for switching play to the weak side (the size depends on the level of the players). The 2 goals with goalkeepers are diagonally opposite.

The white players start on the white cones and the blue players start on the blue cones. On both sides, in the first half the whites have 1 centre back (CB), 1 full back (FB) and 1 central midfielder (CM) - 1 forward (FW1) is in the attacking half and the other forward (FW2) is in the middle zone, as shown. The blue players have a winger (W) and central midfielder (CM) in the first half and a full back (FB) and centre back (CB) in the other half.

The practice runs on both sides simultaneously and starts when the coach passes to the white CB. The white team practice different solutions, altering their decision making to the situation:

- **Scenario 1 (Left Side):** Both blue defenders move to contest white FW1 and FB, which creates a 4 v 4 situation. The white team have no free player to move the ball to within this half, but the blue centre back's movement creates space in behind for FW2. A long aerial pass is played and FW2 can receive and score.

- **Scenario 2 (Right Side):** The blue winger closes down the ball carrier, so FW1 drops back to create a 4 v 3 advantage. The white team exploit this situation to move the ball to the free player (FB). They then have a 3 v 2 or 2 v 1 advantage for an attack in the attacking half and try to score with the help of FW2.

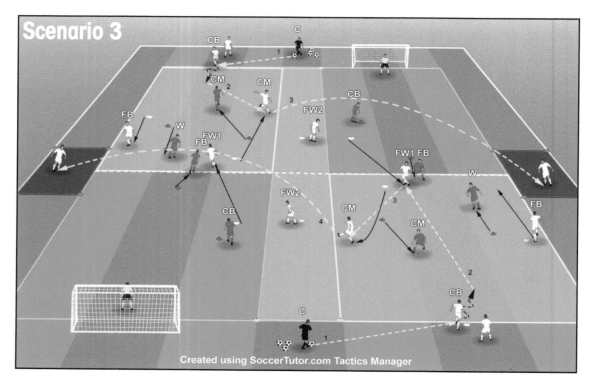

Created using SoccerTutor.com Tactics Manager

- **Scenario 3 (Left & Right Side):** In this situation, the blue winger (W) does not close down the white centre back (CB) - instead he retains balance (wider position) to mark the full back (FB). Also, the blue centre back (CB) in the other half retains his position to mark white FW2. This means that the free white player is now the central midfielder (CM) who has space to receive and then switch the play to the full back on the weak side (white player within small red side zone).

The coach can ask players to either rotate or keep their positions. FW1 and FW2 can keep switching positions throughout either way.

The practice can be reversed to train players on the left side too.

Instructions

1. One white player can move from the first half into the attacking half to help the 2 forwards.
2. For the blues, only the centre back and full back can move freely between the 2 halves.
3. The players inside the small red side zones switch positions with other outside players regularly.

Coaching Points

1. It is important for the defender in possession (CB) to read the tactical situation and make the right decision according to the reactions of the opponents (exploit the 4 v 3 or find a solution for the 4 v 4).
2. The reaction of the opposing winger is key to the defender's decision.

PROGRESSION

3. Creating and Exploiting Space Within a 4 v 3 or 4 v 4 Situation Near the Sideline in a Zonal Game

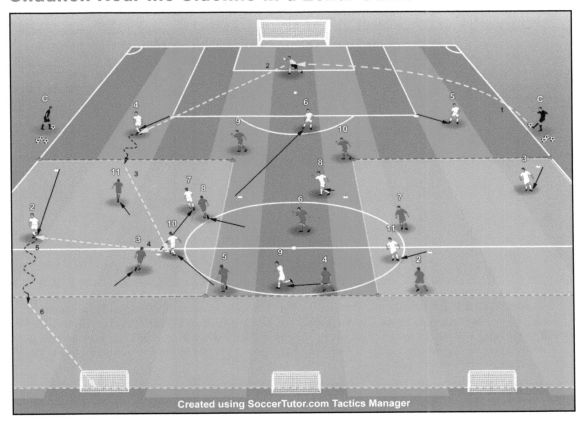

Created using SoccerTutor.com Tactics Manager

Description

Using 2/3 of a full pitch, we mark out 3 zones as shown in the diagram. There is 1 full size goal with a goalkeeper at one end and 3 small goals at the other end.

The practice always starts when the coach plays a long ball towards the goalkeeper and the players adjust their shape to build up play against 2 forwards - Bielsa's 3-4-3 is the example. The 2 centre backs (4 & 5) move out wide to receive, the central midfielder (6) moves back to create a back three and the full backs (2 & 3) push up.

When the goalkeeper passes to one of the centre backs (No.4 in diagram), he moves into the zone on that side as shown. The white team's decision making will depend on the following potential reactions of the blue team:

1. The blue winger (11) closes down the ball carrier and the whites have a 4 v 3 advantage. The white team exploit this situation to move the ball to the free player (No.2) via the 'link player' No.10. The full back (2) can then dribble through the red line into the end zone and score *(as shown in the diagram)*.

2. The blue centre back (5) moves forward to mark No.10, which creates a 4 v 4 situation. This also creates space for a long aerial pass to the white forward (9) who makes a run in behind, receives in the end zone and scores.

3. The blue central midfielder (8) closes down the ball carrier so the winger (11) can mark the white full back (2). This leaves white No.7 free to receive in space and then switch the play to the weak side towards the white left back (3).

The aim for the white team throughout this practice is to use the correct decision making, as explained, and then score in the following ways:

1. Dribble the ball through the red end line.

2. Make a successful pass towards one of the forwards who should receive within the end zone (25 x full width of pitch), without being offside.

The different options and combinations are fully explained in the previous practice and are again applied here.

The blues team's aim is to defend and win possession inside one of the side zones. If they achieve this, they launch a counter attack with the aim of dribbling the ball through the red end line or receiving a pass beyond it, before then scoring in the goal past the goalkeeper (within 8-10 seconds).

Restrictions

1. Only the winger (No.11 in diagram), the full back (3), the central midfielder (8) and centre back (5) on that specific side are allowed to enter the side zone. If it was on the other side of the pitch it would be blue No.7, No.2, No.6 and No.4.

2. The blue players are not allowed to defend beyond the red line (in the end zone).

Coaching Points

1. It is important for the defender in possession to read the tactical situation and make the right decision, according to the reactions of the opponents (exploit the 4 v 3 or find a solution for the 4 v 4).

2. The reaction of the opposing winger is key to the defender's decision.

PROGRESSION

4. Creating and Exploiting Space Within a 4 v 3 or 4 v 4 Situation Near the Sideline in an 11 v 11 Game

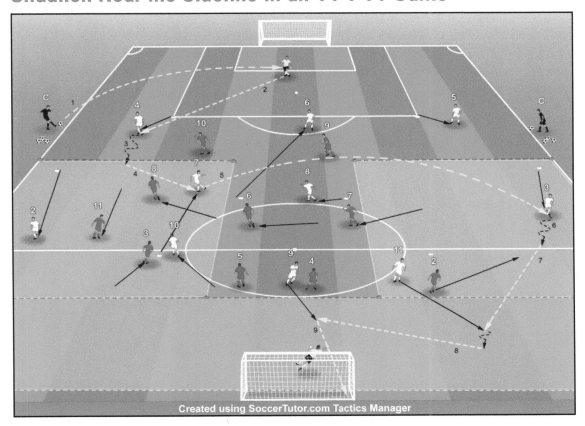

Created using SoccerTutor.com Tactics Manager

Description

This is a progression of the previous practice - we now play an 11 v 11 game.

The exact same objectives, rules and restrictions apply, except the white team must now score in a full sized goal with a goalkeeper. This means that they are more likely to pass/cross from wide positions to score, as shown in the diagram.

The different options and combinations are fully explained in the previous practices and are again applied here.

In the diagram example, No.7 becomes the free player as the white team create a 4 v 3 advantage in the side zone. This enables No.7 to switch the play with a long pass to the left back (3) who has available space to receive and move forward.

CHAPTER 7

BUILDING UP PLAY AGAINST ULTRA-OFFENSIVE PRESSING

BUILDING UP PLAY AGAINST ULTRA-OFFENSIVE PRESSING

Positioning for Bielsa's Defensive 3-4-3 Option vs Ultra-Offensive Pressing with 2 Forwards

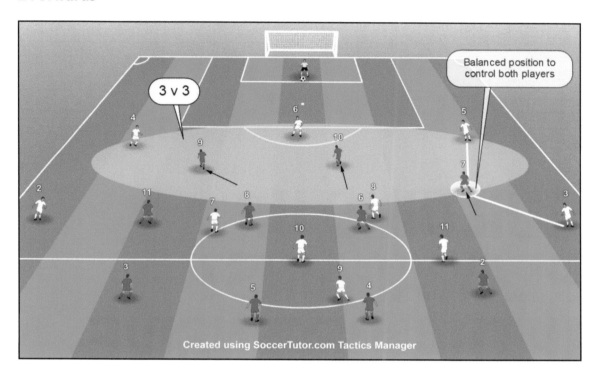

If the opposition have 2 forwards e.g. 4-4-2 formation and apply ultra-offensive pressing in order to force the attacking team to use long balls, one of the wingers (No.7 in diagram) moves into an advanced and balanced position to control both the full back (3) and centre back (5) on that side. At the same time, the forwards (9 & 10) reduce their distance from No.4 and No.6 who are potential receivers of a short pass from the goalkeeper.

The blue right winger (7) can apply immediate pressure on No.5 if the pass is directed to him by the goalkeeper and he can close down the left back No.3 (by taking advantage of the transmission phase), if the goalkeeper directs a long pass to him. This means that the opposition retain their balance and we must find a solution.

ASSESSMENT:

It is better to use Bielsa's more defensive minded 3-4-3 formation when building up play against ultra-offensive pressing (rather than his attacking 3-3-3-1), as we have two players in central midfield (7 & 8) who can act as 'link players' - we can then make it easier to move the ball to the free full backs (2 & 3).

Opposition Winger Blocks the Pass to Our Full Back

As soon as the ball is passed from the goalkeeper to No.5, the blue opposition winger (7) moves to put pressure on him in a way that prevents the direct pass to the left back No.3.

Although No.3 is blocked from receiving the next pass, he stays completely free of marking.

The Ball is Moved to the Free Full Back Through a 'Link Player'

The solution to break through the pressure is to use a 'link player' to move the ball to the free full back No.3.

The central midfielder (8) and No.11 are in suitable positions to become 'link players'. They can both move towards the passing lane to receive and direct the ball to No.3, as shown in diagram.

The 'Link Player' is Marked and the Passing Lane Narrows

If the opposition's central midfielder (blue No.6) is able to shift across in time and mark white No.8 and the passing lane becomes narrow, it becomes too risky to try and use either of the 2 'link players' to move the ball to the free full back (3).

The solution is shown in the next diagram.

Overcoming Pressure by Playing Back to GK + Long Pass Towards the Full Back

The ball is passed back to the goalkeeper and he plays a long pass towards the full back (3).

The ball is directed towards an area where we can exploit a 2 v 1 situation.

If the opposition right back (2) attempts to intercept the long ball and fails, there are many possibilities for our left winger (11) to receive in behind him.

Positioning for Bielsa's Defensive 3-4-3 Option vs Ultra-Offensive Pressing with 1 Forward

Created using SoccerTutor.com Tactics Manager

If the opposition have 1 forward e.g. 4-2-3-1 formation and apply ultra-offensive pressing in order to force the attacking team (whites) to use long balls, both the blue wingers (7 & 11) move into a balanced position to control the centre backs (4 & 5) and the full backs (2 & 3) at the same time.

The blue wingers (7 & 11) can apply immediate pressure on No.4 or No.5 if the pass is directed to them by the goalkeeper and they can close down the white full backs No.2 or No.3 (by taking advantage of the transmission phase), if the goalkeeper directs a long pass to either of them. This means that the opposition retain their balance and we must find a solution.

The blue forward (9) controls our No.6 and a 3 v 3 situation is created at the back.

ASSESSMENT:

The strategies provided on pages 113-114 can also be used as solutions against teams that play with 1 forward, but using 'link players' will be more difficult as the opposition now have an extra man in central midfield - this could mean that white No.7 or No.8 may have to drop deeper to receive.

SESSION 9

Based on Tactics of
Marcelo Bielsa

Building Up Play Against Ultra-Offensive Pressing

SESSION FOR THIS TACTICAL SITUATION (3 PRACTICES)
1. Quick Combination Play to Break Through Ultra-Offensive Pressing & Receive in Behind an Opponent (Unopposed)

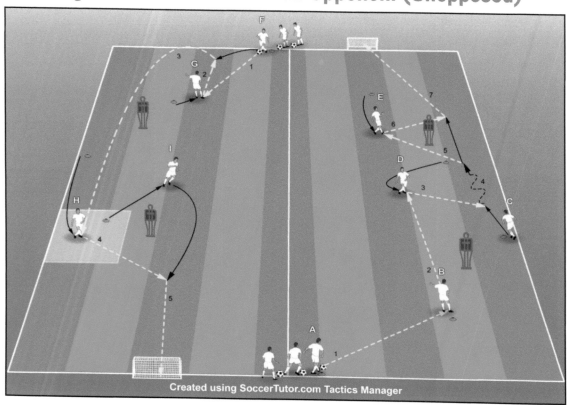

Objective: Technical training to practice moving the ball and receiving behind an opponent in 2 different ways.

Description

In a 30 x 50 yard area, we split the pitch in half and both sides play simultaneously. Each side has 2 mannequins and a small goal, as shown. The left side also has an area for H to receive (size depends on age/level of players).

Right: A passes to B and when B receives, D drops back towards an available passing lane and C moves forward. The ball is directed to C via D who acts as 'link player'. C receives, dribbles forward and plays a 1-2 combination with E, before passing into the small goal. All players move one position forward (A -> B -> C -> D -> E -> F).

Left: F plays a 1-2 combination with G, I drops back towards an available passing lane and H moves forward. F plays a long pass for H to receive on the run within the marked area, while player I makes a curved run behind the mannequin to offer a passing option in behind. H passes to I who passes into the small goal (F -> G -> H -> I -> A).

Coaching Points

1. Players need to use quick combination play - synchronised movements and good passing accuracy.
2. The aim of the practice is to move the ball to the player (C / H) behind the defender (mannequin).

PROGRESSION

2. Breaking Through Ultra-Offensive Pressing On One Side of the Pitch in an 8 (+GK) v 8 Game

Description

Using 2/3 of a full pitch, we mark out a white zone and a yellow zone as shown. The white team have a keeper in a full sized goal and the blue team defend 2 small goals. All of the players have their starting positions marked out with cones. Only the players who are on the strong side after the goalkeeper's pass take part in the practice.

The practice starts with the coach's long pass to the goalkeeper. As soon as the goalkeeper receives the ball, the players adjust their formation to build up against 2 forwards. One of the central midfielders (6) drops back to create a 3 man defence, the centre backs (4 & 5) move wide to receive and the full backs move forward.

The blue forwards move to control two of the three players at the back. One of the blue wingers (No.11 in diagram) follows the white full back (2), while the other one (7) takes up a balanced position to control both the white centre back (5) and the full back (3).

As soon as the goalkeeper passes to a free centre back (No.5 in diagram), the blue winger (7) enters the white zone to create a 3 v 3 situation and win possession. The white team try to overcome the pressure and move the ball to the full back (3) who is free of marking. The aim then becomes to receive inside the yellow zone and score.

Scenario 1: There is an available passing lane to white No.11 who acts as a link player to pass the ball to No.3.

Scenario 2: In this second example (diagram 2b above), there is no available passing lane to white No.11. The white centre back (5) is under pressure and passes back to the goalkeeper. The goalkeeper then plays a long pass to the full back (3) as he is the free player and can receive in space. The white team then have a 2 v 1 situation with a great chance to score.

The white players can either dribble the ball into the yellow zone or receive a pass inside it. In the diagram example, the white team exploit this 2 v 1 situation with No.3 playing a pass in behind for No.11 to run onto, receive within the yellow zone and score.

If the blues win possession, they try to score against the white team's goalkeeper within 8-10 seconds.

Restrictions

1. Only the players who are on the strong side after the goalkeeper's pass take part in the practice. Take turns playing on each side.

2. The blue players are not allowed to enter the yellow zone at any point.

Coaching Points

1. Players need to read the tactical situation and demonstrate good decision making, using quick combination play and synchronised movements.

2. The reading of the positioning of the blue central midfielder (No.8 in diagram) who may block the pass to the 'link player' is key to success in this practice. If he is positioned centrally, the ball can be passed to the white winger *(diagram 2a)* and if he shifts across, the ball should be played back to the goalkeeper *(diagram 2b)*.

PROGRESSION

3. Breaking Through Ultra-Offensive Pressing in an 11 v 11 Zonal Game

Created using SoccerTutor.com Tactics Manager

Objective: The players work on building up play against a team using ultra-offensive pressing and more specifically, on moving the ball to the free full back positioned behind an opponent.

Description

This is a progression of the previous practice within the same area. The same rules and restrictions exist except the pitch is no longer split in half and all the players take part. The two teams play an 11 v 11 game.

The practice starts with the coach's long pass to the goalkeeper. As soon as the goalkeeper receives the ball, the players adjust their formation to build up against 2 forwards. One of the central midfielders (6) drops back to create a 3 man defence, the centre backs (4 & 5) move wider to receive and the full backs (2 & 3) move forward.

The blue forwards (9 & 10) move to control two of the three players at the back. One of the blue wingers (No.11 in diagram) follows the white full back (2), while the other one (7) takes up a balanced position to control both the white centre back (5) and the full back (3).

As soon as the goalkeeper passes to a free centre back (No.5), the blue winger (7) enters the white zone to create a 3 v 3 situation and win possession. The white team try to overcome ultra-offensive pressing and move the ball

to the free full back (3), either through a 'link player' or with a long ball (see previous practice for both options).

The aim then becomes to receive inside the yellow zone and score. The white players can either dribble the ball into the yellow zone or receive a pass inside it. In the diagram example, the white team exploit a 2 v 1 situation after the left back (3) receives the long pass from the goalkeeper. No.3 plays a pass in behind for No.11 to run onto and receive within the yellow zone.

The white team now have to score past the goalkeeper once in the yellow end zone - this will lead to more passes and crosses to finish, as shown in the diagram.

If the blues win possession, they try to score within 8-10 seconds.

Coaching Points

1. Players need to read the tactical situation and demonstrate good decision making, using quick combination play and synchronised movements.

2. The reading of the positioning of the blue central midfielder (No.8 in diagram) who may block the pass to the 'link player' is key to success in this practice. If he is positioned centrally, the ball can be passed to the white winger *(diagram 2a)* and if he shifts across, the ball should be played back to the goalkeeper *(diagram 2b)*.